FREE STUFF
FOR EVERYONE
MADE E-Z

Matthew Lesko

MADE E-Z PRODUCTS, Inc.
Deerfield Beach, Florida / www.MadeE-Z.com

Free Stuff For Everyone Made E-Z™
© 2000 Made E-Z Products, Inc.
Printed in the United States of America

MADE E-Z
PRODUCTS

384 South Military Trail
Deerfield Beach, FL 33442
Tel. 954-480-8933
Fax 954-480-8906

http://www.MadeE-Z.com

2 3 4 5 6 7 8 9 10   CPC   R   10 9 8 7 6 5 4 3 2

Free Stuff For Everyone Made E-Z™
Matthew Lesko

Limited warranty and disclaimer

This self-help product is intended to be used by the consumer for his/her own benefit. It may not be reproduced in whole or in part, resold or used for commercial purposes without written permission from the publisher.

This product is designed to provide authoritative and accurate information in regard to the subject matter covered. However, the accuracy of the information is not guaranteed, as laws and regulations may change or be subject to differing interpretations. Consequently, you may be responsible for following alternative procedures, or using material different from those supplied with this product.

Neither the author, publisher, distributor nor retailer are engaged in rendering legal, accounting or other professional services. Accordingly, the publisher, author, distributor and retailer shall have neither liability nor responsibility to any party for any loss or damage caused or alleged to be caused by the use of this product.

Copyright notice

The purchaser of this guide is hereby authorized to reproduce in any form or by any means, electronic or mechanical, including photocopying, all forms and documents contained in this guide, provided it is for non-profit, educational or private use. Such reproduction requires no further permission from the publisher and/or payment of any permission fee.

The reproduction of any form or document in any other publication intended for sale is prohibited without the written permission of the publisher. Publication for non-profit use should provide proper attribution to Made E-Z Products.

Table of contents

Introduction to Free Stuff For Everyone Made E-Z™

Who doesn't love free stuff?

Times are tough, and we're all looking for more ways to save a few bucks, right? So here are more than 1,000 freebies and cheapies to get you started. They are not all free; only 923 of them are. The rest cost less than $10! But they're well worth it.

Actually, we could have made the book one million and one freebies because the government is so huge that it has at least that many great freebies to offer taxpayers. Remember, these freebies are not really free—you already paid for them with your tax dollars.

What we've done here is put together the government's greatest hits. It's all the neat stuff you can get your hands on and put to use for gifts, self-help, teaching aids, toys, investment decisions and more. Every member of the family can use these freebies.

For Grandma:

- Turn her home into that little bed and breakfast she always wanted.
- Publications that can make her the next "Queen of the Dancing Grannies."

For Mom:

- A "Top Gun" pilot as the featured speaker for her next women's club meeting.
- Break into the world of business with help from the

Women's Business Ownership program.

- Check lead levels in house paint and water to see if it's safe to go home again.

For Dad:

- Extra money reporting the neighborhood tax cheat to the IRS.
- Beat a speeding ticket with a report from the National Institute of Standards and Technology.
- Get a raise, using information from the Bureau of Labor Statistics.

For the kids:

- Dig up real dinosaur bones with some help from the National Park Service.
- Convince mom pizza is good for you with studies from the Food and Nutrition Information Center.

For your mother-in-law:

- Send her to the moon as a NASA civilian astronaut.
- Send her on a free trip to Jamaica as a Peace Corps volunteer.

For Grandpa:

- Let Bill and Hillary send him his next birthday card.
- Make him the life of the party with a free videotape of his prostate surgery.

For your church:

- A free drug-confiscated limousine from the General Services Administration.
- A thousand free books to sell at your next yard sale from the Library of Congress.

For your boss:

- Close down your office until they replace that smelly copier with help from the Environmental Protection Agency.
- Warn him that if he makes a pass at you at the office Christmas party, you and your friends at the Equal Employment Opportunity Commission will see him in court.

For yourself:

- Let the Bureau of the Census point you in the direction of single men and women.
- Let the National Park Service find the best place for you to escape that rat race next summer.

• Have the IRS show you how to write off your vacation expenses.

We all have our limits

Despite our best efforts to make the information in this book as timely and accurate as possible, it is sure to be outdated by the time it reaches your hands. Government policies change every day; and supplies of some items are limited. But you can use this to your advantage.

If the item or publication you call about is no longer available, ask if they have anything new. You may be amazed at what you find. Our researchers, for example, called one department to ask about a publication on commodities trading, only to be told that it was no longer in print. The department, however, offered three more up-to-date booklets and a new information hotline.

If you call one of the numbers listed in this book and find that you have reached the Chinese laundry now using a phone number once assigned to the Department of Commerce, try calling the federal information directory at 202-555-1212. Another good source for phone numbers is the Federal Information Center in your state.

Dealing with bureaucrats: Ten basic telephone tips

An important part of your success in using this book is the careful handling of bureaucrats. Whether you are dealing with your local power company or with the government, you will be speaking to other human beings. If you deal with them pleasantly and patiently, you will get quicker service and more publications and information.

Here are a few important tips to follow when you attempt to get information of any kind from a government agency over the telephone. Above all, remember that patience is often rewarded—even by weary government bureaucrats!

1) *Introduce yourself cheerfully*

Starting the conversation with a cordial and upbeat attitude will set the tone for the entire interview. Let the official know that this is not going to be just another mundane telephone call, but a pleasant interlude in an otherwise hectic day.

2) *Be open and candid*

Be as candid as possible with your source. If you are evasive or deceitful in explaining your needs or motives, your source will be reluctant to provide you with anything but the most basic information.

3) *Be optimistic*

Relay a sense of confidence throughout the conversation. If you call and say "You probably aren't the right person" or "You don't have any information, do you?", it's easy for the person to respond, "You're right, I can't help you." A positive attitude encourages your source to dig deeper for an answer to your question.

4) *Be courteous*

You can be optimistic and still be courteous. Remember the old adage that you can catch more flies with honey than you can with vinegar? Government officials love to tell others what they know, as long as their position of authority is not questioned or threatened.

5) *Be concise*

State your problem simply. Be direct. A long-winded explanation may bore your contact and reduce your chances for getting a thorough response.

6) *Don't be a "gimme"*

A "gimme" is someone who expects instant answers and displays a "give me that" attitude. Be considerate and sensitive to your contact's time, feelings, and eccentricities. Although, as a taxpayer, you may feel you have the right to put this government worker through the mill, that kind of attitude will only cause the contact to give you minimal assistance.

7) *Be complimentary*

This goes hand in hand with being courteous. A well-placed compliment ("Everyone I spoke to said you are the person I need to ask.") about your source's expertise or insight will serve you well. We all like to feel like an "expert" when it comes to doing our job.

8) *Be conversational*

Briefly mention a few irrelevant topics such as the weather or the latest political campaign. The more conversational you are without being too chatty, the more likely your source will be to open up and want to help you.

9) *Return the favor*

You might share with your source information or even gossip you have picked up elsewhere. However, be certain not to betray the trust of either your client or another source. If you do not have any relevant information to share at the moment, call back when you are farther along in your research.

10) *Send thank you notes*

A short note, typed or handwritten, will help ensure that a government official source will be just as cooperative in answering future questions.

For your baby

Chapter 1
For your baby

Are you having a C-section?

The National Institute of Child Health and Human Development can provide data and medical information about this health issue. A 13-page booklet, *Facts About Cesarean Childbirth*, discusses cesarean delivery, types of incisions, current thinking about repeat cesarean, and the pros and cons of this method of birth.

Contact: National Institute of Child Health and Human Development, Building 31, Room 2A32, 9000 Rockville Pike, National Institutes of Health, Bethesda, MD 20892; 301-496-5133; or online at http://www.nih.gov/nichd

Eat for two

Now that you're pregnant, your doctor is going to tell you to gain weight. *All About Eating for Two* is an article describing the types of food and vitamins you will need to maintain a healthy pregnancy.

Once you've had Junior, you have to feed and clothe him. *Feeding Baby: Nature and Nurture and Good Nutrition* and the *High Chair Set* are articles which discuss breast feeding, formula and vitamin supplements.

For your free copies contact: Food and Drug Administration, Division of Consumer Affairs, HFE-88, 5600 Fishers Lane, Rockville, MD 20857; 301-827-4420, 800-532-4440; or online at http://www.fda. gov

Bill welcomes your baby!

The ultimate announcement! Let the president welcome your newest newcomer to the world with a special congratulatory notice sent directly from the White House. Just send a copy of the birth announcement or write a note with the date of birth.

Contact: White House, Greetings Office, 1600 Pennsylvania Ave., NW, Washington, DC 20500; or online at http://www.whitehouse. gov

What if I become diabetic while I'm pregnant?

Understanding Gestational Diabetes: A Practical Guide to a Healthy Pregnancy addresses questions about diet, exercise, measurement of blood sugar levels, and general medical and obstetric care of women with gestational diabetes.

It answers such questions as: Will my baby have diabetes?, What can I do to control gestational diabetes?, Will I have diabetes in the future? This is a free booklet.

Contact: National Institute of Child Health and Human Development, National Institutes of Health, Building 31, Room 2A32, 9000 Rockville Pike, Bethesda, MD 20892; 301-496-5133; or online at http://www.nih.gov/nichd

Pregnancy care

You are pregnant. Now what do you do? How much weight should you gain? Can you keep exercising? The Maternal and Child Health Clearinghouse has several free publications dealing with prenatal care to get you and your unborn child off to a good start.

Some of the publications include:

• *Caring for Our Future: The Content of Prenatal Care* (healthcare professionals).

• *Health Diary: Myself—My Baby*, a new publication which takes you step by step through your pregnancy.

Contact: National Maternal and Child Health Clearinghouse, 2070 Chain Bridge Road, Suite 450, Vienna, VA 22182-2536; or online at http://www.circsol.com/mch

Can I have a drink?

There are many concerns regarding alcohol use while pregnant.

The National Clearinghouse for Alcohol and Drug Information has several free publications dealing with drinking and drug use during pregnancy.

Some of the titles include:

• *How To Take Care of Your Baby Before Birth*, a low-literacy brochure aimed at pregnant women that describes what they should and should not do during their pregnancy, emphasizing a no use of alcohol and other drugs message (PH239, also in Spanish).

- *For a Strong and Healthy Baby* recommends that women do not drink alcohol or use drugs if pregnant or planning to become pregnant (PHD603).

- *Healthy Women/Healthy Lifestyles: Here's What You Should Know about Alcohol, Tobacco and Other Drugs* explains alcohol's effect on women and why women shouldn't drink, smoke or take illicit drugs (PHD691).

- *Pregnant? Drugs and Alcohol Can Hurt Your Unborn Baby* encourages women to talk with someone for more information on stopping substance use (PHD735).

Contact: National Clearinghouse for Alcohol and Drug Information, P.O. Box 2345, Rockville, MD 20847; 800-729-6686; or online at http://www.health.org

Is smoking really dangerous for my unborn baby?

The Office on Smoking and Health can provide you with information on smoking as it affects pregnancy and newborns.

Some of the free pamphlets available include: *Is Your Baby Smoking?*, which explains the dangers of passive smoke on the baby; and a "Pregnant? Two Reasons to Quit" poster, which reminds pregnant women that when they smoke, they smoke for two.

Contact: Office on Smoking and Health, Centers for Disease Control, 4770 Buford Hwy., Mail Stop K-50, Atlanta, GA 30341-3724; 770-488-5705; or online at http://www.cdc.gov/tobacco

Breastfeed or bottlefeed?

Are you debating whether you should breastfeed or bottlefeed? The National Maternal and Child Health Clearinghouse can refer you to several organizations, as well as provide you with free publications dealing with breast feeding, including:

- *Breastfeeding: Consumer Education Materials*, which includes a listing of videotapes, posters, brochures, journal articles, data bases, curricula and training aids.

- *Nutrition During Lactation*, which discusses your diet while you are breastfeeding.

- *Surgeon General's Workshop on Breastfeeding and Human Lactation*, which covers the physiology of breastfeeding, the unique values of human milk, current trends, and cultural factors relating to breastfeeding.

Contact: National Maternal and Child Health Clearinghouse, 2070 Chain Bridge Rd., Suite 450, Vienna, VA 22182-2536; or online at http://www.circsol.com/mch

For your business

Chapter 2

For your business

Flex your time, not your muscles

The U.S. workplace is changing quicker than President Bill's cabinet appointments. Companies have discovered that helping workers with day care and eldercare pays off, and that flexible work schedules mean fewer cases of burnout.

The Work and Family Clearinghouse has written materials and a database where they can match your company with a company of similar needs and geographic area. You can then see how they succeed with these innovative programs.

The Work and Family Resource Kit is a free publication which provides information on all of the above, plus references and resources for further information.

Contact: Work and Family Clearinghouse, Women's Bureau, U.S. Department of Labor, 200 Constitution Ave., NW, Washington, DC 20210; 800-827-5335; or online at http://www.dol.gov/dol/wb

Build a better mousetrap— in Tahiti

Starting up a factory overseas does not make you Benedict Arnold. You can play Albert Schweitzer, and a New Age business guru in many small countries, and still be a good U.S. citizen at home. Learn the best countries to do business in with Foreign Labor Trend reports prepared by American Embassy staff in 70 foreign countries.

Contact: Office of Foreign Relations, U.S. Department of Labor, 200 Constitution Ave., NW., Room S5325, Washington, DC 20210; 202-219-6257; or online at:

http://gatekeeper.dol.gov/dol/ilab/public/aboutilab/org/ofr.htm

Complaint hotline

Need some help resolving a complaint? What about setting up a complaint handling procedure for your business?

The Office of Consumer Affairs works with the business community on behalf of consumers and assists consumers with marketplace problems.

To help businesses improve customer relations and the quality of goods and services, the Office develops cooperative projects with companies, trade and professional associations, consumer organizations, and more. They have many free publications.

- *Business Services Directory* describes business-related activities and services of Commerce Department agencies, and lists telephone numbers for all divisions.

• *Consumer Tip Sheets* are five fact sheets to help consumers resolve their complaints with specific steps to follow for complaints about auto repair, mail order, banking and credit, and travel.

Contact: Office of Consumer Affairs, U.S. Department of Commerce, 14th and Constitution Ave., NW, Room H5718, Washington, DC 20230; 202-482-5001; or online at http://www.doc.gov

From beets to rutabagas

The "AgExport Action Kit" provides information that can help put U.S. exporters in touch quickly and directly with foreign importers of food and agricultural products. The services include trade leads, a Buyer Alert newsletter, foreign buyer lists, and U.S. supplier lists.

Contact: AgExport Connections Staff, U.S. Department of Agriculture, 14th and Independence Ave., SW, Room 4939 South Bldg. Washington, DC 20250; 202-720-7103; or online at http://www. fas.usda.gov/exporter.html

A credit to the gender . . .

If you've been divorced, it can be hard establishing credit, especially if your ex ran up huge credit card bills chasing his lost adolescence. Find out how to restore your good name.

Women and Credit Histories is a free pamphlet that explains your credit rights under the law, how to get help in establishing your own credit, and what to do if you feel your credit application was unfairly denied.

Contact: Public Reference Branch, Federal Trade Commission, 6th and Pennsylvania Ave., NW, Washington, DC 20580; 202-326-2222; or online at http://www.ftc.gov

One glass ceiling is another woman's floor

Do you feel like you are the only woman in town trying to run a business? Ever wonder how you stack up against other businesswomen in the U.S., or whether you should be in another line of work? What about your chances of rising to the top of the heap?

If you're interested in finding out more about women in the workforce, including trends and future projections, you might find the free series of fact sheets on women business owners very interesting.

Some of the topics include:

• *Women and Management*

• *Hot Jobs for the 21st Century*

• *The Family and Medical Leave Act of 1993,* which explains the Act, requirements, and exclusions.

Contact: Women's Bureau, U.S. Department of Labor, 200 Constitution Ave., NW, Room S3311, Washington, DC 20210; 800-827-5335; or online at http://www.dol.gov/dol/wb/

Oh tax-me-not

When the Internal Revenue Service (IRS) knocks, you need a friend, not an accountant.

To make sure you have all your records in order, request Publication 334, *Tax Guide For Small Business*, which explains what can be deducted and how, as well as what records you need to keep.

Contact: Internal Revenue Service, U.S. Department of the Treasury, 1111 Constitution Ave., NW, Washington, DC 20224; 800-829-3676; or online at http://www.irs.gov

Facts on working women

Women will account for 62 percent of the net growth in the labor force over the next ten years.

As part of their free Facts on Working Women series, the Women's Bureau has put together interesting fact sheets including the following:

- *Twenty Facts on Women Workers* examines where women fit into the labor force.

- *Women With Work Disabilities* explains the Americans With Disabilities Act, employment profiles, and employment assistance programs for women.

- *Earnings Differences Between Women and Men* show the earnings gap and the factors that affect it.

Contact: Women's Bureau, U.S. Department of Labor, 200 Constitution Ave., NW, Room S3311, Washington, DC 20210; 800-827-5335; or online at http://www.dol.gov/dol/wb/

Break the glass ceiling

The Glass Ceiling Commission was created to identify artificial barriers that prevent women and minorities from advancing to mid- and upper-level management positions in the corporate world and to determine how such barriers could be removed.

They published a free brochure, *Breaking The Glass Ceiling*, which gives a brief overview of the Commission's work. Also, articles and reports dealing with this issue are available.

The commission has since disbanded, but information may be obtained by contacting: Office of Small Business Programs, U.S. Department of Labor, 200 Constitution Ave., NW, Room C2318, Washington, DC 20210; 202-219-9148; or online at http://www.dol.gov/dol/osbp

The fruitcake's in the mail

Many products are best marketed by mail, but this takes more than stamps and a zip code directory. It takes some knowledge of Federal Trade Commission's Mail Order Rule, which requires companies to ship purchases made by mail when promised or to give consumers the option to cancel their order for a refund.

For a free copy of *A Business Guide to the Mail Order Rule* contact: Federal Trade Commission, 6th and Pennsylvania Ave., NW, Washington, DC 20580; 202-326-2222; or online at http://www.ftc. gov/

Free help finding guardian angels

Look no more. The Investment Division of the U.S. Small Business Administration licenses, regulates, and funds some 283 Small Business Investment Companies (SBIC) nationwide, which supply equity investments to qualifying small businesses.

A free *Directory of Small Business Investment Companies* is available which lists names, addresses, telephone numbers and investment policies of SBICs.

Contact: Investment Division, U.S. Small Business Administration, 409 Third St., SW, Washington, DC 20416; 202-205-6510; or online at http://www.sba. gov

What's hot, what's not

The Federal Procurement Data Center (FPDC) can tell you how much the federal government spent last quarter on products ranging from pasta to real estate.

It also can tell you which agencies made those purchases, and who the contractors were. FPDC summarizes this information through a free, annual standard report, and provides customized reports on a cost recovery basis.

Contact: Federal Procurement Data Center, General Services Administration, 7th and D St., SW, Room 5652, Washington, DC 20407; 202-401-1529; or online at http://fpds.gsa.gov/fpds/ fpds.htm

Is your business in a "sick building"?

Do you suffer from headaches and have difficulty concentrating only while you are at work? You could be working in a "sick building", a term used to describe situations where workers experience acute health or comfort effects when they are at work, but no specific illness can be identified.

The Indoor Air Quality Information Clearinghouse can answer all of your indoor air quality questions and has many free publications on this topic including, *Indoor Air Facts: Sick Building Syndrome.*

Contact: Indoor Air Quality Information Clearinghouse, IAQ INFO, P.O. Box 37133, Washington, DC 20013-7133; 800-438-4318, 202-484-1307; or online at http://www.epa.gov/iaq/

Free consultants make your company a safe and healthy place to work

The Occupational Safety and Health Administration (OSHA) was created to encourage employers and employees to reduce workplace hazards and to implement new or improve existing safety and health programs.

They provide research on innovative ways of dealing with these problems, maintain a recordkeeping system to monitor job-related injuries and illnesses, develop standards and enforce them, as well as establish training programs.

OSHA has an extensive list of publications on a variety of job hazards. Some of the titles include:

- *Asbestos Standard for Construction Industry*

- *Hearing Conservation*

- *Respiratory Protection Program Highlights*, a one-sheet description of hazards, standards, of OSHA programs or policies.

- *Employee Workplace Rights.*

- *How to Prepare for Workplace Emergencies*

Contact: Occupational Safety and Health Administration, U.S. Department of Labor, 200 Constitution Ave., NW, Room N3101, Washington, DC 20210; 202-219-4667; or online at http://www. osha.gov

Go to the bank

Think you don't have the money to start a business? *A Guide To Business Credit For Women, Minorities, and Small Business* is a free publication which describes the various credit opportunities for industrious entrepreneurs. Don't let the lack of funds hold you back.

Contact: Publications Services, MS-127, Federal Reserve Board, Washington, DC 20551; 202-452-3244; or online at http://www.bog.boardfrb. fed.us/pubs/pubs.htm

No money—no problem

Raising capital is a little bit like raising kids; it's a pain, but worth the effort.

How To Start a Small Business is a package of documents outlining the basics of raising money, where to find it, borrow it, types of business loans, how to write a loan proposal, and U.S. Small Business Administration (SBA) financial programs (you'll have to do the kids yourself) .

For your free copy contact: Marketing and Communications, U.S. Small Business Administration, 409 3rd St., SW, Washington DC 20416; 202-205-6744; or online at http://www.sba.gov

Plants eliminate 90% of office pollution

Office plants are great places to hide microphones, but they also clear up 90% of office pollution, according to a National Aeronautics and Space

Administration (NASA) study, called *Interior Landscape Plants for Indoor Air Pollution Abatement*. The study shows that house plants remove chemicals from the air and clean up indoor air pollution.

The report is free from Educator Resource Center, Bldg. 1200, Stennis Space Center, MS 39529; 601-688-3338; or online at: http://www.ssc.nasa.gov

Some nighttime reading

Read every line before you sign. The Federal Trade Commission has a package of publications to help you learn your way around the franchise business.

When you go in for the big meeting, you'll know the right questions to ask.

• *Franchise and Business Opportunities* is a four page guide about what to consider.

• *Franchise Rule Summary* is a seven page explanation of the federal disclosure rule.

For your free copies contact: Federal Trade Commission, Pennsylvania Ave. at 6th St., NW, Washington, DC 20580; 202-326-2220; or online at http://www.ftc.gov/

More than 138 government bulletin boards

That's what the National Technical Information Service (NTIS) Fed World will connect you to. Many government agencies have collected their material in one place and make it available online through this service.

You can order popular government reports, receive specialized information in areas like patent abstracts, and even get information on government studies and research results.

The fees range from free information to $3,000 for an annual subscription, but 95% of the information is free. Call for information about access to the service list: NTIS FED WORLD, 703-487-4608 (voice); or contact them online at http://www.fedworld.gov

Help your employees clean up their own act

Making your workplace clean and safe should also include looking at your employees. Are some coming in late often or not at all? Are there problems with some employees' work habits? It could be that drugs or alcohol are involved.

The National Institute on Drug Abuse is developing programs to eliminate illegal drug use in the workplace. Its programs include research, treatment, training, and prevention activities, as well as projects related to the development of a comprehensive Drug-Free Workplace programs.

The Clearinghouse distributes the following four-part videotape series on drugs at work:

- *Drugs At Work* (employee/employer versions) presents information about the nature and scope of the alcohol and drug problem in the workplace and about the Federal Government's initiative to prevent and reduce the problem ($8.50).

- *Getting Help* (employee/employer versions) highlights the benefits of an effective employee assistance program to employees and employers through comments by business, labor, and government leaders and Employee Assistance Program professionals ($8.50).

- *Drug Testing: Handle With Care* (employee/employer versions) describes the options available for designing a drug testing component as part of a comprehensive drug-free workplace program ($8.50).

- *Finding Solutions* portrays drug abuse in the workplace is portrayed as a community-wide problem. The solutions offered through education and prevention are presented as personal, workplace, and community responsibilities ($8.50).

Contact: National Clearinghouse for Alcohol and Drug Information, P.O. Box 2345, Rockville, MD 20847; 800-729-6686; or online at http://www.health.org

Should my company go public?

If my company becomes public, what do I have to tell? Are there legal ways to sell securities without registering with the Securities and Exchange Commission (SEC)?

The free booklet, *Q&A: Small Business and the SEC* discusses capital formation and the federal securities laws and is designed to help you understand some of the basic necessary requirements that apply when you wish to raise capital by selling securities.

Contact: U.S. Securities and Exchange Commission (SEC), Publications Section, M/SC-11, 450 5th St., NW, Washington, DC 20549; 202-942-4040; or online at http://www.sec.gov

Dial-a-porn business boom

Thinking about getting rich quick by starting a dial-a-porn phone service? Before you do, better make sure you know the federal laws concerning these services and how to comply with them.

For the free fact sheet, *International Dial-A-Porn*, contact: Federal Communications Commission, Consumer Assistance and Small Business Division, Office of Public Affairs, 1919 M St., NW, Room 254, Washington, DC 20554; 202-418-0200; or online at http://www.fcc. gov

Workers' comp for federal employees

Do you work for Uncle Sam and were you injured on the job? *Federal Injury Compensation* is a free publication which lists questions and answers regarding the Federal Employees' Compensation Act. They can also provide you with claim forms and checklists for evidence required in support of claims for occupational diseases.

Contact: Federal Employees' Compensation Division, Office of Workers' Compensation Programs, Employment Standards Administration, U.S. Department of Labor, 200 Constitution Ave., NW, Room S3229, Washington, DC 20210; 202-219-7552; or online at http://www.dol.gov/dol/esa/owcp.htm

Lend a helping hand

Want to help your employees recover from drug or alcohol addiction? Want to institute a "drug-free workplace" program, but aren't sure how?

The National Clearinghouse for Alcohol and Drug Information has several free publications and videos (for $12.50) dealing with drugs and the workplace to get you started. Some of the titles include:

- *An Employer's Guide to Dealing with Substance Abuse* (PHD543)

- *Drug Testing: Handle with Care* (VHS06; $12.50)

- *Working Partners: Substance Abuse in the Workplace* (RPO899)

- *Cost Effectiveness and Preventative Implications of Employee Assistance Programs* (RPO907)

- *Making Your Workplace Drug Free: A Kit for Employers* (WORKIT)

- *America in Jeopardy: The Young Employee in the Workplace* (VHS44; video; $12.50)

Contact: National Clearinghouse for Alcohol and Drug Information, P.O. Box 2345, Rockville, MD 20847; 800-729-6686; or online at http://www.health.org/index.htm

Got a great idea?

Got a great idea that just can't wait? The Patent and Trademark Office administers the patent and trademark laws, examines patent applications, and grants patent protection for qualified inventions.

For more information on what is required for patents and trademarks, several free publications are available including:

- *Basic Facts About Patents*

- *Basic Facts about Trademarks*

- *Disclosure Document Program*

Contact: Public Affairs, Patent and Trademark Office, U.S. Department of Commerce, Washington, DC 20231; 703-308-4357; or online at http://www.uspto.gov

Check out the mail

Even the mail isn't safe anymore. Mail fraud and mail theft seem to be big business. How do you protect yourself, your employees, and your company?

A free booklet, *Postal Crime Prevention: A Business Guide*, shows business owners how to protect themselves from con artists and thieves whose business is mail fraud and mail theft. It includes information on different types of mail fraud, check cashing precautions, guidelines for mailroom security, bombs in the mail, as well as additional information.

Contact your nearest Post Office or: Public Affairs Branch, U.S. Postal Service, 475 L'Enfant Plaza, SW, Room 5541, Washington, DC 20260; 202-268-2284; or online at http://www.usps.gov

Teach your workers English

Want information on workplace or family literacy?

The National Clearinghouse for ESL Literacy Education covers all aspects of literacy education for adults and out-of-school youth learning English as a second language. They publish digests, bibliographies, resource guides and more on the topic.

Free digests include:

• *Workplace ESL Instruction: Varieties and Constraints*

• *Adult ESL Learner Assessment: Purposes and Tools*

• *Union-Sponsored Workplace ESL Instruction*

For more information contact: National Clearinghouse for ESL Literacy Education, Center for Applied Linguistics, 1118 22nd St., NW, Washington, DC 20037; 202-429-9292; or online at http://www. cal.org/ncle

Mom's home office

Starting a home-based business is often an economic necessity, because of the cost of childcare, the desire to be home with the kids, and more.

- *The Business Plan For Home-Based Business* ($4) is a publication of the U.S. Small Business Administration (SBA) and provides a comprehensive approach to developing a business plan for just such a venture. Once you've got your plan, all the rest you need is courage.

- *Selling By Mail Order* ($3) provides basic information on how to run a successful mail order business and includes information on product selection, pricing, testing, and writing effective advertisements.

- *How to Get Started with a Small Business Computer* ($3) helps you forecast your computer needs, evaluate the alternatives and select the right computer system for your business.

To obtain a directory and order form, write SBA Resource Directory, MC 7110, 409 3rd St., SW, Washington, DC 20416; 202-205-6666; or online at http://www.sba.gov

Energy business

The National Energy Information Center is the central distribution point for most U.S. Department of Energy (DOE) publications, including the free *Energy Information Administration Publications Directory: A Users Guide.*

The directory includes current program information sources; an index of DOE, state, and federal agency contacts; a directory of DOE technical information with descriptions of computerized databases and other resources; and more.

For your copy contact: National Energy Information Center, Energy Information Administration, U.S. Department of Energy, 1000 Independence Ave., SW, Room E1-231, Washington, DC 20585; 202-586-8800; or online at http://www.eia.doe.gov

Be your own financial manager

Just make sure you know what you are doing.

The Small Business Administration (SBA) has a series of publications dealing with financial management, designed to educate you on budgeting, money management issues, and record keeping. Some of the titles include:

- *ABCs Of Borrowing* ($3)

- *Understanding Cash Flow* ($3)

- *Financing For Small Business* ($3)

- *Budgeting In A Small Service Firm* ($3)

- *Pricing Your Products and Services Profitably* ($3)

To obtain a directory and order form, write SBA Resource Directory, MC 7110, 409 3rd St., SW, Washington, DC 20416; 202-205-6666; or online at http://www.sba.gov

More than running the cash register

Good employees are worth more than gold. Learn how to find and hire the right employees.

- *Employees: How To Find and Pay Them* ($3) gives you some guidelines for your personnel search.

- *Human Resource Management for Growing Businesses* ($3) uncovers the characteristics of an effective personnel system and training program. Learn how these functions come together to build employee trust and productivity.

To obtain a directory and order form, write SBA Resource Directory, MC 7110, 409 3rd St., SW, Washington, DC 20416; 202-205-6666; or online at http://www.sba.gov

Maternity and family leave

Thirty-four states, Puerto Rico, and the District of Columbia have enacted some form of state maternity/family leave law to meet the changing needs of the American work force.

To find out what states have these laws and the scope of the law, request the free publication, *State Maternity/Family Leave Law*, available through the U.S. Department of Labor's Women's Bureau.

The publication outlines the law for each state, the employees covered by the law, temporary disability insurance, and enforcement or administration of the law for each state.

Contact: Women's Bureau, U.S. Department of Labor, 200 Constitution Ave., NW, Washington, DC 20210; 202-219-6652; or online at http://www.dol.gov/dol/wb/

First, the idea

Inventors are idea people. To help them become business people, the U.S. Small Business Administration (SBA) has several publications on what step two needs to be.

- *Ideas Into Dollars* identifies the main challenges in product development and provides a list of resources to help inventors ($3).

- *Avoiding Patent, Trademark and Copyright Problems* shows how to avoid infringing the rights of others and the importance of protecting yours ($3).

- *Creative Selling: The Competitive Edge* explains how to use creative selling techniques to increase profits ($2).

To obtain a directory and order form, write SBA Resource Directory, MC 7110, 409 3rd St., SW, Washington, DC 20416; 202-205-6666; or online at http://www.sba.gov

Cheap ways to spread the word

Think about getting out the word using bulk mail discounts offered by the U.S. Postal Service. You can find out about using this and other postal discounts by getting free copies of:

- *Designing Business Letter Mail*

- *Designing Reply Mail*

- *Nonprofit Standard Mail Eligibility*

- *How to Find Financing for Your Business*

There are 85 Postal Business Centers across the country set up to provide, at no cost to customers, business building information. Contact: U.S. Postal Service, Advertising Mail, 475 L'Enfant Plaza, SW, Room 5540, Washington, DC 20260; or online at http://www.usps.gov/busctr

What's overtime?

You must pay time and a half to any of your employees who work more than a forty-hour work week. This does include some salaried employees, although there are four groups who are exempt from this requirement: executives, professionals, administrative, and those in the outside sales field. Information is available on what job requirements are necessary for those in the exempt category.

Contact: Wage and Hour Division, Fair Labor Standards, U.S. Department of Labor, 200 Constitution Ave., NW, Room S3516, Washington, DC 20210; 202-219-4907; or online at http://www. dol.gov

Carpal tunnel syndrome

Carpal tunnel syndrome is a tingling sensation in the hands and fingers and can be caused or aggravated by repeated twisting or awkward postures, particularly when combined with high force. The population at risk includes persons employed in such industries or occupations as construction, food preparation, clerical work, product fabrication, and mining.

The National Institute For Occupational Safety and Health (NIOSH) has a publication entitled *Cumulative Trauma Disorders* (95-119), which contains information on carpal tunnel syndrome, including current research, preventive recommendations, a bibliography, and articles.

Contact: National Institute For Occupational Safety and Health, 4676 Columbia Parkway, Cincinnati, OH 45226; 800-356-4674; or online at http://www.cdc.gov/niosh/homepage.html

Help for inner city businesses

Want to help improve your neighborhood that is in a poor section of town? How about starting a business? There are loans available to small businesses owned by low-income persons, or to businesses which are located in an area with a high percentage of unemployment or low-income individuals. The money can be used to establish, preserve or strengthen a business.

Help revitalize your neighborhood. To learn how to apply for the loans and for credit criteria, contact your local Small Business Administration office, or the Small Business Answer Desk, Small Business Administration, 409 Third St., SW, Washington, DC 20416; 800-8-ASK-SBA; or online at http://www.sba.gov

Overseas carryout

Do you have some food you would like to start exporting overseas? The Foreign Agricultural Service (FAS) has the experts in exports.

They have agricultural attaches and counselors stationed around the world who can help you market and sell your products. Some of the free publications they have to offer include:

- *Foreign Market Information Reports*

- *AgExporter*

- *Food and Agricultural Export Directory*

For more information on the services that are available contact: Foreign Agricultural Service, Information Division, U.S. Department of Agriculture, Washington, DC 20250; 202-720-7103; or online at http://www.fas.usda.gov/

Special help for women

Did you know that women-owned businesses fare much better than those run by men?

To help women along, there is a special Office of Women's Business Ownership within the Small Business Administration. They offer grants to local organizations to help women start and maintain their own businesses. These demonstration projects provide services and assistance in the form of financial management, marketing training, and counseling to startup a business or help an established ongoing business.

For more information, contact: Small Business Administration, Office of Women's Business Ownership, 409 Third St., SW, Washington, DC 20416; 202-205-6673; or online at http://www.onlinewbc. org

Have an energy-saving idea?

Help can be just a phone call away. There is a special program for those working on an energy-related invention. The assistance comes in many forms including an evaluation of the invention, limited funding assistance, and maybe even advice concerning engineering, marketing, or business planning. You may petition for a waiver of government patent rights.

For more information contact: Inventions and Innovation Division, Energy-Related Inventions Program (EE-521), U.S. Department of Energy, 820 W. Diamond Ave., Room 264, Gaithersburg, MD 20878; 301-975-5500; or online at http://www.nist.gov/techeval

Money to sell food overseas

The government would love to export more food overseas, but sometimes it takes some work teaching other cultures how to use the food products.

There is money available through the Market Promotion Program. These funds are provided through the Foreign Agricultural Service of the U.S. Department of Agriculture and can only be used to support activities conducted outside the United States. You can use the money for consumer advertising, point of sale demonstrations, public relations, participation in trade fairs, market research, and more.

To learn more about this program contact: Commodity and Marketing Programs, Foreign Agricultural Service, U.S. Department of Agriculture, Washington, DC 20250; 202-720-5521; or online at http://www.fas.usda.gov/

Video display terminals— user friendly?

Over a million people each day sit down to work in front of a terminal, inputting and outputting information.

There have been concerns about the risks these terminals present. Are we destroying people's eyesight? Are they at risk for carpal tunnel syndrome?

The National Institute For Occupational Safety and Health (NIOSH) has put together an information bibliography entitled *Video Display Terminals* describing video display terminals, the current research on their use, and a listing of articles for further information.

Contact: National Institute For Occupational Safety and Health, 4676 Columbia Parkway, Cincinnati, OH 45226; 800-356-4674; or online at http://www.cdc.gov/niosh/homepage.html

MBA without the degree

Your business is up and running, so keep it headed in a good direction with a little help from the Small Business Administration (SBA).

They have publications on management and planning, which can help you look at the decisions you need to make. Some of the publications include:

• *Checklist For Going into Business* ($3)

• *Problems In Managing A Family-Owned Business* ($3)

• *Planning And Goal Setting For Small Business* ($3)

• *Developing a Strategic Business Plan* ($3)

• *Business Plan for Small Service Firms* ($4)

To obtain a directory and order form, write SBA Resources Directory, MC 7110, 409 3rd St., SW, Washington, DC 20416; 202-205-6666; or online at http://www.sba.gov

For your career

Chapter 3

For your career

Check out the headhunters

When you are out looking for that perfect job, you will run into many companies that offer job hunting assistance. The Federal Trade Commission (FTC) often receives complaint letters about job counseling and placement services which charge large fees and misrepresent their services.

They publish two free publications: *Job Ads, Job Scams*, which explains things you need to look out for, and *Job Hunting: Should You Pay*, which explains about headhunter services and things you need to consider before you sign on.

Contact: Federal Trade Commission, Bureau of Consumer Protection, 6th and Pennsylvania Ave., NW, Washington, DC 20580; 202-326-2222; or online at http://www.ftc.gov

Landing an excellent job

Tap the government for tips on finding the best work opportunities. *Tips For Finding The Right Job* helps you to evaluate your interests and skills, and provides information on resumes, application letters, job interviews, and more.

For your free copy contact: Employment and Training Administration, U.S. Department of Labor, 200 Constitution Ave., NW, Room N4700, Washington, DC 20210, 202-219-6871; or online at: http://www.pueblo.gsa.gov/ cic_text/employ/tipjob.txt

Check it out

Want to check out internship possibilities?

The Office of Museum Programs has put together *Internship Opportunities at the Smithsonian Institution* ($5), which is a comprehensive guide to 40 museums and offices at the Smithsonian that offer internships. Although the programs described are directed at the college level and above, this book gives valuable information about museum careers and provides details on the rich variety of research and museum functions at the Smithsonian, which may be of interest to high school students.

Contact: Center for Museum Studies, 900 Jefferson Drive, SW, Room 2235, Washington, DC 20560; 202-357-3103; or online at: http://www.si.edu/ cms/iosi.htm

Get the scoop on dirt

Does a career in archeology or anthropology interest you? Are you a teacher and want to learn more? *Summer Fieldwork Opportunities* is a free survey of opportunities for teachers and students aged 16 and above to participate in summer fieldwork.

Contact: Anthropology Outreach and Public Information Office, National Museum of Natural History, MRC 112, Smithsonian Institution, Washington, DC

20560; 202-357-1592; or online at http://www.mnh.si.edu/nmnhweb.html

Weigh yourself on the salary scale

If you've got the itch to pull up stakes, know your worth wherever you're going by contacting the Bureau of Labor Statistics. They publish the *Occupational Compensation Surveys* which contain information on jobs and salary wages and occupation hourly wage for different cities across the country.

For a copy of a survey contact: Division of Occupational Pay and Employee Benefit Level, Office of Compensation and Working Conditions, Bureau of Labor Statistics, U.S. Department of Labor, Postal Square Bldg., Room 4160, 2 Massachusetts Ave., NE, Washington, DC 20212, 202-606-6220; or online at http://stats.bls.gov/ocshome.htm

Is Jacques Cousteau your idol?

Thinking about a career in oceanography? The Department of Vertebrate Zoology has a free bibliography and listing of sources entitled *Careers in Biology, Conservation, and Oceanography* which can help you learn about the various fields you are considering.

Contact: National Museum of Natural History, Department of Vertebrate Zoology, Room 369, MRC 109, Smithsonian Institution, Washington, DC 20560; 202-357-2740; or online at http://www.mnh.si.edu/nmnhweb.html

Turn off the Weather Channel

Think you can do better than the weatherman? Study hard and a career could be in the making. You can learn a great deal about the weather from the

National Weather Service. They have free publications covering every weather condition imaginable from floods to tornadoes. Some of the freebies include:

• *Hurricane Tracking Chart*

• *Spotter's Guide for Identifying and Reporting Severe Local Storms*

• *Hurricane! A Familiarization Booklet*

• *Are You Ready For a Tornado?*

• *Mariner's Guide to Marine Weather Services*

• *Key to Manual Weather Observations and Forecasts*

• *Atlantic Hurricane Tracking Map*

For information about the publications and more, contact Customer Service Corps, National Weather Service, 1325 East-West Highway, Silver Spring, MD 20910; 301-713-0622; or online at http://www.nws.noaa.gov/om/

Solar power

A career in an efficient energy field might be just what you need. The Energy Efficiency and Renewable Energy Clearinghouse has free publications which deal with a variety of renewable energies technologies. They have *Educational Materials for Teachers and Students: High School*, and one for those in college. These should provide enough information to get you started in your studies.

For these publications and more, contact: Energy Efficiency and

Renewable Energy Clearinghouse, P.O. Box 3048, Merrifield, VA 22116; 800-363-3732; or online at http://www.eren.doe.gov

Stay in school

The Student Educational Employment Program is designed to provide Federal employment for financially needy students that attend high school or a post-secondary institution. Every effort is made to assign students to positions that are career related or of interest to the full-time student. Students work part-time during school and/or full-time during the summer. Salary is based on work experience and education.

To get additional information and qualifications contact the Federal agency employment office where you are interested in working, or: U.S. Office of Personnel Management, Washington Area Service Center, 1900 E St., NW, Washington, DC 20415; 202-606-1800; or online at: http://www.usajobs.opm.gov/

Put your mouth to work

Has your mouth gotten you into some trouble or does it make you the hit of parties? You could be a natural for a job as a DJ. Most disc jockeys need to be licensed, so get a licensing application packet from the Federal Communications Commission.

Contact: Federal Communications Commission, 1919 M St., NW, Washington, DC 20554; 800-418-3676; or online at http://www.fcc.gov

Check out the options

Don't waste four years of college to get a degree that won't get you a job.

Check out the job market through a series of Bureau of Labor Statistics publications titled *Occupational Outlook Handbook* reprints.

The series is broken down into various occupational groupings, and outlines degrees needed, job availability forecast, and even in what area of the country the demand for you will be highest. There are 20 different reprints which include:

- *Tomorrow's Jobs: Overview* (029-001-03276-5; new)

- *Business and Managerial Occupations* (029- 001-03225-1; $3.50)

- *Computer and Mathematics-Related Occupations* (029-001-03227-7; $1.75)

- *Health Technologists and Techniques* (029- 001-03232-3; $1.50)

- *Clerical and Other Administrative Support Occupations* (029-001-03288-9; new)

- *Sales Occupations* (029-001-03235-8; $1.75)

- *Engineering, Scientific, and Related Occupations* (029-001-03226-9; $2.50)

You can order your reprint (or a complete set for $24) from Superintendent of Documents, Government Printing Office, Washington, DC 20402; 202-512-1800; or online at http://www.gpo.gov

Co-op with the experts

The Peace Corps offers a Cooperative Education Program which is designed to give students paid work experience in their academic field of study.

Students must be enrolled on a full-time basis in their school's Cooperative Education Program. In addition, they must be working towards a degree, whether it be high school, undergraduate, graduate or professional.

For more specific information, contact: Office of Human Resource Management, Peace Corps, 1990 K St., NW, Suite 4100, Washington, DC 20526; 202-606-3038; or online at http://www.peacecorps.gov

Volunteer

The Volunteer Service Program offers unpaid work experience to students who are in high school or college. You will get academic credit for the work that you perform. Most students will be involved in professional projects and activities.

The projects could involve research on environmental concerns or congressional issues. Most students work three to four months during the school year or the summer. You must contact the federal agency you would like to work with directly.

For additional information on the program, contact the personnel office at the federal agency or department for which you wish to work (look in the blue pages of your phone book under "Federal Government"). You may also contact: U.S. Office of Personnel Management, Washington Area Service Center, 1900 E St., NW, Washington, DC 20415; 202-606-1800; or online at http://www.usajobs.opm.gov/b1p.htm

Don't be tied to a desk

If the outdoors is where you want to be, then look into a profession where hiking boots are part of the uniform. *A Challenge and An Adventure* is a free loan video that describes the various kinds of work the Fish and

Wildlife Service is involved in. This could be the key to your future.

To borrow a copy contact your regional office, or for information regarding the office nearest you: Office of Public Affairs, Fish and Wildlife Service, U.S. Department of Interior, Washington DC 20240; 202-208-5611, or fax a written request to 202-208-7409. You can also contact them online at http://www.fws.gov

Fly right

Thinking of a career in aviation?

For every one pilot, there are 1500 other aviation professionals supporting operations on the ground.

To help you learn more about the aviation field, the Federal Aviation Administration has several publications which outline the various careers, technical requirements, and educational backgrounds. Some of the titles include:

- *Aviation Careers: The Sky's The Limit* (050-007-01112-1; $6.50)

- *Directory of Transportation Education: A Quick Reference Guide* (050-007-01111-3; $5)

- *Aviation Education Resource Centers* (050-007-01106-7; $2)

To order, contact Superintendent of Documents, U.S. Government Printing Office, Washington, DC 20402; 202-512-1800. Some of these documents are also available free on the Internet. Connect to FEDIX at http://web.fie.com/

Work for the CIA

The Central Intelligence Agency (CIA) offers four different Student Programs.

Each program has specific qualifications and benefits, and gives practical hands-on experience and work in a field that pertains to the student's area of study such as: graphic design, languages, economics, printing/photography and more. The programs are as follows:

- **Undergraduate Scholar Program**—offers graduating high school students, especially minorities and individuals with disabilities who have a financial need for tuition assistance, the opportunity to work in a challenging position every summer through college.

- **CIA Summer Intern Program**—provides students the opportunity to gain good work experience during the summer while making a competitive salary. Employment starts the summer of the student's sophomore year.

- **Undergraduate Student Trainee Program**—gives practical experience in combination with academic studies. Individuals will also receive a competitive salary. As part of the program, work is alternated with school on a semester or quarterly basis.

- **Graduate Studies Program**—available to students entering their first or second year of graduate school, students are given the opportunity to work at the professional level and receive a competitive salary. Usually internships are in the summer, but some are available other times.

For more information on the various programs contact: Central Intelligence Agency Personnel Representative, P.O. Box 12727, Arlington, VA 22209-8727; 800-336-2163; or online at: http://www.odci.gov/cia/index.html

Your job magazine

Want to figure out what's happening on the career front? Get a subscription for only $9.50 to the *Occupational Outlook Quarterly* (729-008-00000-1) which covers such topics as job training, internships, profiles of workers, and matching personal and job characteristics.

There is also information on how to get a federal job and occupational projections to the year 2005.

For your subscription contact: Superintendent of Documents, Government Printing Office, Washington, DC 20402; 202-512-1800; or online at http://www.gpo.gov

Gone fishin'

The Fish and Wildlife Service has a Student Career Experience Program that is available in Washington as well as in the different regions.

The program is very competitive but gives students the opportunity to get paid while working and learning.

Students can be undergraduate or graduate and are assigned based on their academic studies or career goals. Positions can be administrative or technical depending on your expertise and their availability.

For more information contact: U.S. Fish and Wildlife Service, Chief Office of Human Resources, 4401 N. Fairfax Dr., Webb 300, Arlington, VA 22203; 703-358-1724; or online at http://www.fws.gov/~r9ohr/hp_scep.html

Reach for the stars

No need to stay on the ground when the sky is

the limit. *Careers in Aerospace* can give you an idea of the choices and options you have if you always dream of the stars.

For your free copy contact: National Aeronautics and Space Administration, Publication Center, Code FE-02, Washington, DC 20546; 202-554-4380; or online at http://www.nasa.gov

For some direction

Career decision making and career change are affecting more and more people as the job market seems to be changing.

The ERIC Clearinghouse for Adult, Career, and Vocational Education covers all areas of career and vocational/technical education from basic literacy training through professional skill upgrading.

Although they cannot tell you what career is best for you, they can provide you with a series of free ERIC Digests to help you look at the job market in a variety of ways. Some of the titles they have include:

• *Job Search Methods*

• *Adults in Career Transition*

• *Jobs In the Future*

• *Locating Job Information*

For your copies or for more information contact: ERIC Clearinghouse for Adult, Career, and Vocational Education, The Ohio State University, 1900 Kenny Rd., Columbus, OH 43210; 800-848-4815; or online at http://www.ed.gov/pubs/pubdb.html

Astronaut training

If you always wanted to be an astronaut, then this book is for you. *Astronaut Selection and Training* gives a basic overview of the requirements, steps and stages one must complete before becoming an astronaut. Historical information is supplied as well.

Free from: National Aeronautics and Space Administration Educational Publications, Code FE-02, Washington, DC 20546; 202-554-4380; or online at http://www.nasa.gov

Energy education

Education has always been an important part of the U.S. Department of Energy's mission. The National Energy Information Center coordinates education programs and resources within the U.S. Department of Energy. The free publication *Energy Education Resources* details U.S. Department of Energy resources at the K-12 level. It also contains a list of the National Laboratories run by or affiliated with the U.S. Department of Energy and the education programs they sponsor.

For your free copy contact: National Energy Information Center, EI-30 Energy Information Administration, Forrestal Building, Room 1F-048, 1000 Independence Ave., SW, Washington, DC 20585; 202-586-8800; or online at http://www.eia.doe.gov

Defense work

The U.S. Department of Defense offers two different programs through the Office of the Secretary of Defense (OSD). Security clearance is needed in order to work for the Defense Department and can take four to six months, so apply early.

These programs are:

- **Salaried Internships**—available through the Washington Headquarters Services which fills the personnel needs of OSD. The positions are usually announced in December by the Office of Personnel Management (202-632-7484).

- **Unsalaried Internships**—available throughout the year based on the needs of OSD.

For more information write: Human Resource Service Center, U.S. Department of Defense, AMC Building, Room 2N36, Attn: Diana Hall, 5001 Eisenhower Ave., Alexandria, VA 22333; 703-617-7178; or online at http://www.hrsc.osd.mil/train.htm

$3,000 to design a stamp

If you are an artist who has a great idea for a postage stamp, the U.S. Postal Service might pay you to design one—$3,000 for a single stamp.

First you will need to have your work reviewed by their staff, and if they like your stuff, they might hire you as a freelancer to do a stamp.

Contact: Stamp Marketing Division, Office of Philatelic and Retail Services, U.S. Postal Service, 475 L'Enfant Plaza, Room 4461-E, Washington, DC 20260-6810; 202-268-7700; or online at http://www.usps.gov

A matter of national security

The National Security Agency (NSA) has a Cooperative Education Program that gives students responsibility right from the start.

The Co-op Program is based on a series of semester-long "work tours." They are planned, supervised experiences with increased responsibilities each time. The projects will also be different each tour, which gives you the opportunity to try new things.

The four main disciplines are: electrical or computer engineering, computer science, languages, and mathematics.

For more information contact: National Security Agency, Attention M322 Co-op (FAE), Fort Meade, MD 20755-6000; 800-962-9398; or online at http://www.nsa.gov

Free instructions

The Mine Safety and Health Administration is responsible for the safety and health of our mines, and has a *Catalog of Training Programs For the Mining Industry*, which contains free instructional programs. Although these programs focus on mining, they are not exclusive to this field.

Some of the programs include:

• *Cement: On-The-Job Training Modules*

• *First Aid Book*

• *Mining Accident Prevention*

• *Underground Coal: On-The-Job Training Modules*

For a copy of your free catalog contact: Office of Information and Public Affairs, Mine Safety and Health Administration, U.S. Department of Labor, 4015 Wilson Blvd., Room 601, Arlington, VA 22203; 703-235-1452; or online at http://www.msha.gov

Join the team

Be a mover and a shaker.

The Presidential Management Internship Program (PMI) is an entry level career development and training program designed to attract outstanding men and women to careers in public service. If chosen to be a PMI, one would be a part of a very challenging two-year program.

You will participate in training conferences, seminars, and Congressional briefings, and will have the opportunity to learn at an accelerated pace and sharpen your management and leadership skills. PMIs are rotated to different federal agencies to get additional experience. Opportunities are also available in regions outside of Washington.

Contact: Office of Personnel Management, Philadelphia Service Center, William J. Green Federal Bldg., 600 Arch St., Philadelphia, PA 19106; 215-597-1920; or online at http://www.usajobs.opm.gov/b3.htm

Practice MBA

Get a step ahead of other business students. The Financial Management Service of the U.S. Department of the Treasury offers the Cooperative Education Program. The type of positions available are in the areas of computer systems, finance, business administration, and accounting with students assigned based on their major. In addition to getting good experience you will receive a competitive salary.

For more information write: U.S. Department of the Treasury, Financial Management Service, Cooperative Education Coordinator, 401 Fourteenth St., SW, Washington, DC 20227; 202-874-7090; or online at http://www.fms.treas.gov

Bank on it

The world of high finance may be for you. The Export Import Bank

(EXIM Bank) has opportunities for college students to get valuable experience working in an international banking atmosphere. The bank has Student Volunteer Internship Programs which are offered throughout the year. The student is assigned a mentor and either analyzes data or works on special projects.

For more information contact: Director of Human Resources, Export Import Bank of the United States, Suite 1005, 811 Vermont Ave., NW, Washington, DC 20571; 202-565-3327; or online at http://www.exim.gov

Energize

The U.S. Department of Energy offers the Undergraduate Research Participation Program in many of its different agencies and administrations. The student will be given the opportunity to work in an area of expertise, usually in engineering, sciences, and business.

In the area of business, a co-op would be doing accounting, finance, or general business. Another possibility would be in the area of science, where a co-op would be doing computer work or physics.

For more information contact: U.S. Department of Energy, Special Employment Programs Team, 1000 Independence Ave., SW, Room 4H080, Washington, DC 20585; 202-586-7231; or online at: http://www.sandia.gov/esteem/home.html

20 occupations most desired by feds

Looking for a job, but can't seem to find anything? The Bureau of Labor Statistics has a free report, *Twenty Occupations For Which the Largest Number of College Graduates Were Hired*, from the summer 1993

Occupational Outlook Quarterly on the 20 occupations most often hired by the federal government. If yours happens to be one of those, maybe it's time for you to think of working for Uncle Sam.

Contact: Bureau of Labor Statistics, U.S. Department of Labor, Washington, DC 20212; 202-606-5691.

Women doing the jobs of men

It's no longer necessary for women to settle for low paying, dead-end jobs at fast food restaurants and offices.

More and more, women are landing good paying jobs at what used to be traditionally only male jobs, such as: carpenters, electricians, masons, plumbers, auto mechanics, welders, and so on. *The Directory of Non-Traditional Training and Employment Programs Serving Women* (029-002-00080-1; $9) outlines many of the free training programs all across the country for women interested in landing these "male" jobs.

Contact: Superintendent of Documents, Government Printing Office, Washington, DC 20402; 202-512-1800; or online at http://www.gpo.gov

Free job training for teens

You don't have to pay to go to an expensive trade school to learn how to become a welder, mechanic, nurses aide, or even a draftsman. If you're a low-income teen, you may qualify for free training through the Job Corps. There's even help getting your GED. You can find out what Job Corps programs are available in your area and elsewhere. Free publications include:

Job Corps in Brief, Train for Your Future, and *Job Corps:A Chance To Make It.*

Contact: Office of Job Corps, U.S. Department of Labor, 1333 H St., NW, Suite 300 West, Washington, DC 20005; 800-733-JOBS; or online at http://www.jobcorps.org/

Does a college degree guarantee a job?

A recent report from the Bureau of Labor Statistics shows that a college degree will not guarantee you a job after graduation, nor will it even guarantee you a job that requires a college degree.

The free report *The College Labor Market: Outlook, Current Situation, and Earnings* is reprinted from the summer 1994 issue of the *Occupational Outlook Quarterly.*

Contact: Bureau of Labor Statistics, U.S. Department of Labor, Washington, DC 20212; 202-606-5691.

The list of lists

The federal government offers a wide variety of internships to undergraduate and graduate students. You can find out about the possibilities by contacting the Employment or Human Services Office of the federal agencies.

Rep. Mel Watt of North Carolina has also put together a web page with a collection of internship opportunities. Over 115 programs and contacts are listed, from Amtrak to the USIA. Take a look at http://www.house. gov/watt/intern.htm

For your community

Chapter 4

For your community

Neighborhood watch

Worried about safety in your neighborhood and considering trying to get a neighborhood watch program started?

The National Institute of Justice has free information on community policing programs which involve the police force making their presence known by increased foot patrols and other services.

Contact: National Institute of Justice, NCJRS, Box 6000, Dept. AID, Rockville, MD 20850; 800-851-3420, 301-519-5500; or online at h t t p : / / w w w . o j p . usdoj.gov/nij/

Consumer resource

A free *Consumer's Resource Handbook* shows you how to communicate more effectively with manufacturers, retailers and service providers.

The first section features tips on avoiding purchasing problems and getting the most for your money by giving steps for handling your own complaint and writing an effective complaint letter. The second section, the Consumer Assistance Directory, lists consumer offices in both public and private sectors that provide assistance for consumer complaints. Handbooks are available by written request.

Contact: Handbook Publication Request, U.S. Consumer Product Safety Commission, Washington, DC 20207. You can also contact the Consumer Information Center, Pueblo, CO 81009; 719-948-4000; or online at http://www.pueblo.gsa.gov/1977res.htm

Clean up the air in your part of the world

Fuel efficiency is something important to consider when buying a new car. The gas tax will affect you less, and your car will run more efficiently. The U.S. Environmental Protection Agency publishes a free annual Mileage Guide which contains fuel economy estimates for all new makes and models. Peruse the list before you hit the showrooms.

Contact: Public Information Center 3404, U.S. Environmental Protection Agency, 401 M St., SW, Washington, DC 20460; 800-363-3732; or online at http://www.epa.gov/omswww.mpg.htm

Chemicals in your community— learn what you need to know

Congress passed a law designed to help America's communities deal safely and effectively with the many hazardous substances that are used throughout our society.

The law is called the Emergency Planning and Community Right-to-Know Act; and this booklet has been written to help you understand and take advantage of your rights and opportunities under this far-reaching law.

The first part of the guide describes how the law works, what its provisions were intended to accomplish, and how all members of the community can play an active part in making sure the law is carried out. The second part discusses specific groups and organizations affected by the law, describes what they can do or are required to do to make it work, and tells how they can benefit from it.

Contact: Public Information Center 3404, U.S. Environmental Protection Agency, 401 M St., SW, Washington, DC 20460; 800-553-7672; or online at http://www.epa.gov/epahome/publicat.htm

Is it safe to drink the water?

The Safe Drinking Water Hotline can answer any question or concern you may have regarding drinking water, and provide you with publications. Some of the free publications they have include:

• *Home Water Testing*

• *Bottled Water Fact Sheet*

• *Lead In Your Drinking Water*

• *List of National Primary Drinking Water Regulations Fact Sheet*

Contact: Safe Drinking Water Hotline, U.S. Environmental Protection Agency, 401 M St., SW, Washington, DC 20460; 800-426-4791; or online at http://www.epa.gov/ogwdw/pubs/

Recycling efforts

Landfills are overflowing and now is the time to take action. *Recycling Works!* is a free booklet that provides information about successful recycling programs initiated by state and local agencies. It also describes private recycling efforts and joint recycling ventures of government and businesses.

Contact: Resource Conservation and Recovery Act Hotline, U.S. Environmental Protection Agency, 401 M St., SW, Washington, DC 20460; 800-424-9346; or online at: http://www.epa.gov/epaoswer/non_hw/recycle/index.htm

Changed your oil lately?

We all know that we are supposed to change oil regularly in our car, and many of us do it ourselves to save money. But what do we do with the old oil? Can you throw it in the sewer?

Oil is a valuable resource when properly recycled. Recycling can conserve our nation's natural resources, protect the environment, and save consumers money. However, when improperly disposed of, used oil can contaminate the soil and surface and ground waters.

The Resource Conservation and Recovery Act (RCRA) Hotline has several free publications dealing with recycling used oil including:

- *How to Set Up Local Programs to Recycle Used Oil*

- *Collecting Used Oil: Tips for Consumers Who Change Their Own Oil*

- *Managing Used Oil: Advice for Small Businesses*

• *Recycling Used Oil:What Can You Do?*

Contact: RCRA Hotline, U.S. Environmental Protection Agency, 401 M St., SW, Washington, DC 20460; 800-424-9346, 703-412-9810; or online at http://www.epa.gov/epaoswer/hotline/index.htm

Clean the air

There is help close to home for your indoor air concerns. *The Inside Story:A Guide to Indoor Air Quality* describes sources of air pollution in the home and office, corrective strategies, and specific measures for reducing pollutant levels. This illustrated booklet covers all major sources of pollution such as radon, household chemicals, biological contaminants, carbon monoxide, formaldehyde, pesticides, asbestos, and lead. This includes a glossary and a list of sources for additional information.

This free directory is available from: Indoor Air Quality Information Clearinghouse, P.O. Box 37133, Washington, DC 20013; 800-438-4318; or online at http://www.epa.gov/iaq/

Bringing art to life

The National Gallery of Art's Extension Program is an attempt to develop awareness of the visual arts and make its collections accessible to everyone, no matter how far away from the Gallery they may live.

The programs are loaned free of charge to educational institutions, community groups, and to individuals throughout the United States.

Nearly 150 programs are offered in a variety of mediums, including slides, videos, films, and video-discs, and cover specific topics or time periods.

The slide sets usually come with an audiocassette and text. A complete catalog of programs is available at no charge from the Extension Programs Office.

Some of the programs include:

Slide Sets:

- "Survey of American Painting"

- "Famous Men and Women in Portrai

- "Introduction to Understanding Ar

- "African Art"

- "Impressionism"

Videos:

- "The Christmas Story in Art"

- "Leonardo: To Know How To See"

- "The Eye of Thomas Jefferson"

- "John James Audubon: The Birds of America"

- "Matisse in Nice"

- "Art of Indonesia"

Contact: Department of Education Resources, Education Division, National Gallery of Art, 4th St. and Constitution Ave., NW, Washington, DC 20565; 202-842-6273; or online at http://www.nga.gov/resources/ep-index.htm

Base closure catastrophe

With cutbacks in defense, bases are being closed all across the country. The Office of Economic Adjustment assists local communities, areas or states affected by U.S. Department of Defense actions, such as base closures, establishment of new installations, and cutbacks or expansion of activities. It publishes a number of free publications on these issues, including: *Communities in Transition*, and *Planning for Civilian Reuse of Former Military Bases*.

For these publications or additional information for communities concerned about base closings contact: Office of Economic Adjustment, U.S. Department of Defense, 400 Army Navy Dr., Suite 200, Arlington, VA 22202; 703-604-5689; or online at http://emissary.acq.osd.mil/bctoweb/home.nsf

Cushion the blow

Air bags are a more complicated issue than they used to be. Are they safe for you? What about for your children?

The National Highway Traffic Safety Administration (NHTSA) has put together a number of reports, fact sheets, and brochures on air bags and air bag safety. Find out about installing an on-off switch, air bag injury statistics, child passenger safety steps, and more.

Publications available include:

• *How to Get an Off On Switch*

• *Survey of Driver Seating Positions in Relation to the Steering Wheel*

• *Kids and Air Bags: It's as Easy as 1-2-3*

• *Air Bag Safety Fact Sheet*

Contact: National Highway Traffic Safety Administration, 400 Seventh St., SW, Washington, DC 20590; 800-424-9393 (Auto Safety Hotline), or online at http://www.nhtsa.dot.gov/airbags/

Look within to help your town

Tired of seeing troubled youths hanging out? What about lonely or bored senior citizens? The Corporation for National and Community Service is Uncle Sam's domestic volunteer agency and supports many programs designed to provide lasting solutions to the challenges of crime, hunger, poverty, illiteracy, drug abuse, and homelessness.

If you or your organization are looking for ways to improve your community, look to the Corporation for help. Some of their programs include Volunteers in Service to America (VISTA), the Foster Grandparent Program, the Retired Senior Volunteer Program, the Senior Companion Program, the Student Community Service Program, and the Program Demonstration and Development Division.

Contact: Corporation for National and Community Service, 1201 New York Ave., NW, Washington, DC 20525; 202-606-5000; or online at http://www.nationalservice.org

Stop crime

One of the fastest growing, most visible crime control programs in the United States is Crime Stoppers, also known as Crime Solvers, Secret Witness, Crime Line, or other names. These self-sustaining programs join the news media, the community, and law enforcement as an alliance to involve private citizens in the fight against serious crime.

Crime Stoppers—A National Evaluation is a free publication which describes these programs, their effectiveness, and more. For your copy contact: National Institute of Justice Clearinghouse, NCJRS, Box 6000. Dept. AID, Rockville, MD 20850; 800-851-3420; or online at http://www.ncjrs.org

Performance arts

The Education Department of the John F. Kennedy Center for the Performing Arts has a wide variety of programs and services for individuals, schools and communities interested in the arts. From the Performing Arts Centers and Schools: Partners in Education programs to Opportunities for Young Performers, the Kennedy Center is a great place to look for arts education.

One outstanding document is the "Cuesheet", which is a collection of performing arts study guides published by the Education Department and the National Symphony Orchestra (NSO). Cuesheets are designed for teachers' use before and after attending performances for school groups and families at the Kennedy Center. Cuesheets are wonderful resources containing introductory information and activities appropriate for all children, even without experiencing the performance. Some sample cuesheets include:

• *Alice in Wonderland* (theater)

• *Walking the Winds: American Tales* (theater)

• *Lakota Sioux: Indian Dance Theatre* (dance)

• *NSO Young People's Concerts: An American Adventure* (music)

Contact: Performing Arts Centers and Schools Program, Education Department, The Kennedy Center, Washington, DC 20566; 202-416-8822; or online at http://artsedge.kennedy-center.org/cuesheet/

Wetlands protection

What are wetlands and why are they important? The U.S. Environmental Protection Agency's (EPA) Wetlands Protection Hotline is responsive to public interest, questions and requests for information about wetlands, and options for their protection.

The hotline can provide you with many free publications on the topic.

- *Wetlands Protection: A Local Government Handbook* is available which reviews federal and state laws and programs that promote wetlands preservation.

- *Protecting America's Wetlands* outlines President Clinton's focus on wetlands protection. The Hotline also has a packet of 32 fact sheets which cover a variety of topics relating to wetlands including information on the Clean Water Act, EPA's regional offices, as well as general information on the importance of wetlands.

Contact: Wetlands Protection Hotline, Labat-Anderson Inc., Mail Code 4502F, Washington, DC 20460; 800-832-7828; or online at:

http://www.epa.gov/owow

The endangered species hit list

Most people know that the California condor and the bald eagle are on the endangered species list, and the spotted owl saga has been on the front page a great deal.

The U.S. Fish and Wildlife Service has a free series of one page biologues on a variety of endangered species, including the three listed above.

They also can provide you with the Endangered Species Act, a copy of the Federal Register titled *Endangered and Threatened Wildlife and Plants*, and an informational brochure, *Endangered Species*.

For your copies, contact: Fish and Wildlife Service, Publications Unit, Mail Stop 130 Arlsq., U.S. Department of Interior, Washington, DC 20240; 703-358-1711; or online at http://www.fws.gov.

Don Quixote would be proud

Windmills are not a thing of the past, but a thing of the future. The U.S. Department of Energy's Wind Energy Program assists utilities and industry in developing advanced wind turbine technology to be economically competitive.

The Energy Efficiency and Renewable Energy Clearinghouse has several free publications which describe wind energy programs, such as:

• *Wind System Installation Legal and Safety*

• *Small Wind Energy Systems for the Homeowner*

• *Wind Energy C Small Scale Systems*

For these publications and more information on wind energy, contact: Energy Efficiency and Renewable Energy Clearinghouse, P.O. Box 3048, Merrifield, VA 22116; 800-363-3732; or online at: http://www.erecbbs.nciinc.com

In your neighborhood

The Cooperative Extension Service, part of the U.S. Department of Agriculture, uses research, knowledge, and educational programs to assist people in making practical decisions. Its mission is to help people improve their lives through an educational process that uses scientific knowledge focused on issues and needs.

Located in almost every county across America, the Cooperative Extension Service provides information on topics ranging from diet to finances, from families to farming. Most of the information provided at the local level is free or low cost. *Patterns Of Change* outlines the plan for the future of the Service.

For your free copies or for information about an office near you, contact: Cooperative State Research Education and Extension Service, U.S. Department of Agriculture, Room 3328, Washington, DC 20250; 202-720-3029; or online at http://www.reeusda.gov/

Get rid of the town dump

You can help your town learn how to better get rid of waste by using the latest methods of source reduction, recycling, composting, planning, and even education, legislation, and public participation.

There's a clearinghouse that helps individuals, industries, and state and local governments keep up on the latest methods of coping with waste.

Contact: The RCRA Hotline, U.S. Environmental Protection Agency, 401 M St., SW, Washington, DC 20460; 800-424-9346; or online at: http://www.epa.gov/epaoswer/non-hw/recycle/index.htm

Clean it up

Tired of all the pollution? It's time for you to act and learn how to reduce, reuse, and recycle.

- *The Consumer's Handbook for Reducing Solid Waste* describes how individual consumers can help alleviate the mounting trash problem by making environmentally aware decisions about everyday things like shopping and caring for the lawn.

- *What You Can Do To Reduce Air Pollution* explains the major air pollutants, the goals of the Clean Air Act, and the actions you can take to reduce pollution.

Both are free from the National Center for Environmental Publications and Information, P.O. Box 42419, Cincinnati, OH 45242; 800-490-9198; or online at http://www.epa.gov/ncepihorn/

Environmental awareness

Communities are becoming more aware of the need to take a close look at the demands they place upon their environment. Recycling is becoming more prevalent. Conservation is taking place, and communities are examining other types of energy such as solar.

The Energy Efficiency and Renewable Energy Clearinghouse has a series of publications and fact sheets on a variety of energy related topics, such as:

• *Selecting a New Water Heater*

• *Landscaping for Energy Efficiency*

• *A Guide to Making Energy-Smart Purchases*

• *Cooling Your Home Naturally*

• *Energy Efficiency for Cities and Counties*

For your free copies or more information on the topic contact: Energy Efficiency and Renewable Energy Clearinghouse, P.O. Box 3048, Merrifield, VA 22116; 800-363-3732; or online at http://www.eren.doe.gov

Roadside improvements

Make your neighborhood a cleaner, safer place to live with some help from the Federal Highway Administration.

They publish a variety of brochures, reports, and guides which provide information on highway safety.

Some of the titles include:

• *Read Your Road: Every Highway User's Guide to Driving Safely*

• *Roadside Improvements for Local Roads and Streets*

• *Guide to Safety Features for Local Roads and Streets*

• *Fatal and Accident Rates on Public Roads in the United States*

For your free copies contact: Federal Highway Administration, Office of Highway Safety (HHS-1), 400 7th St., SW, Washington, DC 20590; 202-366-0660;

or online at http://www.ohs.fhwa.dot.gov

Cable catastrophe

Is your cable bill going up yet again? Who regulates the cable companies? The Federal Communications Commission (FCC) can provide you with the facts.

- *FCC Fact Sheet on the Public's Role in Cable Rate Regulation*, explains basic cable service rates and where you need to complain regarding the rates.

- *Fact Sheet on Cable Carriage of Broadcast Stations* explains a new cable law which requires cable systems to receive a station's permission to carry them.

- *General Cable Television Industry and Regulation Information Fact Sheet* provides consumers, cable companies, and other interested parties with information on cable regulation.

You can use this service to find out how to file complaints, learn about cable programs that have been dropped, and to obtain copies of cable forms, cable rules, and regulations.

For more information contact: Federal Communications Commission, General Cable Inquiries, P.O. Box 18698, Washington, DC 20036; 202-418-7096; or online at http://www.fcc.gov

For your diet

Chapter 5

For your diet

Don't let your cooking make you ill

You have probably heard on the news about a recent *e coli* scare. The U.S. Department of Agriculture and the FDA have joined together to form the Foodborne Illness Education Information Center, which provides information about foodborne illness prevention to educators, trainers and consumers. Its purpose is to increase the knowledge of food related risks from production through consumption, and has developed two education databases which contain consumer and food worker educational materials.

To learn more on how you can prevent foodborne illness, contact: USDA/FDA Foodborne Illness Education Information Center, National Agricultural Library/USDA, Beltsville, MD 20805; or online at http://www.nal.usda.gov/fnic/foodborne/foodborn.htm

When eating is a problem

Over 3% of girls and young adult women suffer from anorexia and bulimia. Learn the dangers of these illnesses, symptoms, treatments, how to help, and resources for more information. Request the free publication, *Eating Disorders*, and help your loved one on the road to good health.

Contact: National Institute of Mental Health, Room 7C-02, 5600 Fishers Lane, Rockville, MD 20857; 301-443-4513; or online at: http://www.nimh. nih.gov

Some dinner reading

For books on nutrition, the Food and Nutrition Information Center offers *Nutri-Topics* which are free brief reading lists designed to help locate information or resources on a given topic.

They are available as separate lists of resources appropriate for one or more user levels: consumer, educator, and health professional. Included are print materials, videos, journal articles, pamphlets, and lists of contacts for further information. Topics include:

• *Nutrition and Cancer*

• *Consumer Resource List on Food Allergies and Intolerances*

• *Food and Nutrition Fun For Kids*

• *Nutrition and Cardiovascular Disease*

• *Nutrition and Diabetes*

• *Nutrition and the Elderly*

• *Food Composition*

• *Resources About Eating Disorders for Consumers*

• *Herbal Medicine*

• *Sensible Nutrition*

• *Sports Nutrition*

• *Vegetarian Nutrition*

• *Weight Control*

Contact: Food and Nutrition Information Center, U.S. Department of Agriculture, National Agricultural Library, Room 304, 10301 Baltimore Blvd., Beltsville, MD 20705; 301-504-5719; or online at: http://www.nalusda. gov/fnic/index.html

Are the kids and I eating right?

The National Maternal and Child Health Clearinghouse has several free publications concerned with pregnancy and early childhood nutrition:

• *Nutrition During Pregnancy: Weight Gain, Nutrient Supplements*

• *Nutrition and Your Health: Dietary Guidelines for Americans*

• *Healthy Foods: Healthy Baby*

Contact: National Maternal and Child Health Clearinghouse, 2070 Chainbridge Rd., Suite 450, Vienna, VA 22182-2536; or online at http://www.circsol.com/mch/

Eating right to lower cholesterol and high blood pressure

Has your doctor told you that your cholesterol is too high? What about your blood pressure? You may be on medication, or maybe your doctor has suggested a change in lifestyle to help your condition.

The Information Center for the National Heart, Lung, and Blood Institute can answer your questions regarding cholesterol, high blood pressure and heart disease.

They can provide you with free journal articles, and other information on these topics, including several publications dealing with nutrition such as:

• *Check Your Cholesterol and Heart Disease I.Q.*

• *Protect Your Heart—Lower Your Blood Cholesterol*

• *Controlling High Blood Pressure: A Woman's Guide*

• *Stay Active and Feel Better*

• *Take Steps—Prevent High Blood Pressure*

• *Step by Step: Eating to Lower Your High Blood Cholesterol*

Contact: Information Center, National Heart, Lung, and Blood Institute, P.O. Box 30105, Bethesda, MD 20824; 301-251-1222; or online at http://www. nhlbi.nih.gov/nhlbi/nhlbi.htm

The fountain of food

One of the Food and Drug Administration's (FDA) missions is to protect the safety and wholesomeness of food. They regulate what's termed fresh, what's low fat, and more.

They test samples of food to see if any substances, such as pesticide residues, are present in unacceptable amounts. If contaminants are identified, FDA takes corrective action.

FDA also sets labeling standards to help consumers know what is in the foods they buy. Information is available (for free) on a wide variety of topics including, but not limited to: calcium and other special needs of women, cellulite removal gimmicks, eating disorders, fad diets and diet books, fast food and nutrition, food preparation, nutrition labels, organic foods, saccharin, salt, vitamins.

Contact: Information Office Of Consumer Affairs, Food and Drug Administration, 5600 Fishers Lane, Rockville, MD 20857; 800-532-4440, 301-827-4420; or online at http://www.fda.gov

Information for community nutrition services

The National Clearinghouse for Primary Care Information offers manuals for community health centers, primary care providers, home health services, HMOs, and outpatient clinics on approaches for establishing a nutrition program.

Single copies of a 96-page *Guide for Developing Nutrition Services in Community Health Programs* is available free, and covers the planning, developing, and evaluating of nutrition services as an integral component of community health programs.

Contact: National Clearinghouse for Primary Care Information, 8201 Greensboro Dr., #600, McLean, VA 22102; 703-821-8955; or online at http://158.72.85.159/

Know what the most informed people know

The Food and Nutrition Information Center is a great starting place for every nutrition question you have. They can send you free information, refer you to videos, books, articles, print materials, or other resources on your topic of interest. Some of the materials include:

- *Nutrition Education Printed Materials and Audiovisuals:* Grades Preschool through 6

- *Nutrition Education Printed Materials and Audiovisuals:* Grades 7-12

- *Database of Food and Nutrition Software and Multimedia Programs*

- *Nutrition Education Resource Guide: An Annotated Bibliography of Educational Materials for the WIC and CSF Programs*

- *Sources of Free or Low-Cost Food and Nutrition Materials*

Contact: Food and Nutrition Information Center, U.S. Department of Agriculture, National Agricultural Library, Room 304, 10301 Baltimore Blvd., Beltsville, MD 20705; 301-504-5719; or online at http://www.nalusda. gov/fnic/index.html

The road to good health

...starts with a good diet. One day you're told to eat carbohydrates, the next day it's fruit. Get the facts from the people who wrote the book on nutrition. The Food and Drug Administration (FDA) has several free publications which can help you eat right and enjoy the good life.

- *Women and Nutrition: A Menu of Special Needs*

• *A Consumer Guide to Fats*

• *Fiber: Something Healthy To Chew On*

• *Dietary Guidelines For Americans*

• *Olestra and Other Food Substitutes*

For these and other publications on food, contact: Food and Drug Administration, Division of Consumer Affairs, HFE-88, 5600 Fishers Lane, Rockville, MD 20857; 800-532-4440, 301-827-4420; or online at http://www.fda.gov

Talk turkey

Actually, you can talk about any meat or poultry product with the experts at the U.S. Department of Agriculture's Meat and Poultry Hotline.

They can answer your questions regarding power outages, meat and poultry labels, cooking time, and meat safety.

Some of the publications they have to offer include:

• *Turkey Basics: Safe Cooking*

• *A Quick Consumer Guide to Safe Food Handling*

• *Talking About Turkey*

• *A Consumer's Guide to Safe Food Handling of Ground Meat and Poultry*

For more information on meat and poultry items contact: Food Safety and Inspection Service, U.S. Department of Agriculture, Washington, DC 20250; 800-535-4555; or online at http://www.usda.gov/fsis

Change the channel

Plug in these videos and turn on a healthy alternative to chips and dip. Discover how to make food taste great without fat, salt, and all the other no-nos.

The Food and Nutrition Center has three publications to get you started:

- *Audiovisuals About Low Fat, Low Cholesterol Eating for a Healthy Heart*

- *Audiovisuals About Weight Control*

- *Audiovisuals About Basic Nutrition*

To receive these publications, send a self-addressed, stamped envelope with 64 cents postage to: Food and Nutrition Information Center, National Agricultural Library, Room 304, 10301 Baltimore Blvd., Beltsville, MD 20705; or online at http://www.nalusda.gov/fnic/index.html

There never is an easy way out

Heard the one about the cream that makes fat go away? Seems like it is on every drug store shelf, but that doesn't mean it really works.

The Food and Drug Administration (FDA) is aware of the use of aminophylline and xanthine derivatives in thigh cream. They are currently evaluating the status of these types of products and labeling claims being made for them. The agency has not approved these products. They are marketed solely at the responsibility of the manufacturer or distributor.

For more information on this product you can contact your area FDA office or the Compliance Division, Over-The-Counter Drugs, Center for Drug Evaluation and Research, FDA, HFD-312, 5600 Fishers Lane, Rockville, MD 20857; 301-594-1065; or online at http://www.fda.gov/cder

For your education (college survival guide)

6

Chapter 6

For your education (college survival guide)

Crash course in college economics

Preparing Your Child for College: A Resource Book for Parents will help you eliminate your fear that you won't be able to afford to send your kids to college. This free resource book shows that college can really be for everyone.

Contact: Office of Planning and Evaluation Service, U.S. Department of Education, 400 Maryland Ave., SW, Washington, DC 20202; 800-827-5327 (Information Resource Center), 800-433-3243 (Student Aid Info Line); or online at http://www.ed.gov/pubs/prepare/

Birth control or self-control

The locker room is no place to research contraception, tips on safe sex, or whether college is a good place to start a family. Get the facts on contraception. The Office of Population Affairs has brochures and pamphlets on family planning, adolescent abstinence, and adoption.

Some of the titles include *Your Contraceptive Choices* which examines the various birth control methods and *Many Teens Are Saying No (sex)*, which promotes the benefits of abstinence.

Contact: Office of Population Affairs Clearinghouse, P.O. Box 30686, Bethesda, MD 20824; 301-654-6190; or online at http://www.dhhs.gov/progorg/opa/clearing.html

The GI Bill

If you have served in active duty or in the reserves, you may be eligible for education benefits under the Montgomery GI Bill.

The Veterans Benefits Administration publishes two free booklets titled *Summary of Education Benefits Under the Montgomery GI Bill-Active Duty Educational Assistance Program, Chapter 30 of Title 38 U.S. Code* and *Summary of Educational Benefits Under the Montgomery GI Bill-Selected Reserve Educational Assistance Program, Chapter 106 of Title 10 U.S. Code.* Both booklets contain information on eligibility and benefits.

Contact: Veterans Benefits Administration, U.S. Department of Veterans Affairs, 810 Vermont Ave., NW, Washington, DC 20420; 800-827-1000; or online at http://www.va.gov/vas.index1.htm

What's a pound worth?

Does a fad diet seem the only way to chop those excess pounds? Lose weight safely and effectively. *Facts About Weight Loss* is a free publication which helps you avoid deceptive weight loss programs, potentially harmful pills, and phony devices or gadgets.

Contact: Center for Food Safety and Applied Nutrition, 200 C St., SW, Washington, DC 20204; 800-532-4440; or online at http://vm.cfsan. fda.gov/list.html

Speed trap 101

Caught speeding on your way to school? What about drinking and driving? The report, *Police Traffic Radar*, published in February, 1980, is still accurate and shows that all police radar tracking devices are not accurate all of the time. Such evidence can be helpful in the defense of your case.

This laboratory also has information regarding alcohol breath testing devices, including *Breath Alcohol Sampling Simulator for Qualification Testing of Breath Alcohol Measurement Devices*. Both publications are free.

Contact: Office of Law Enforcement Standards, National Institute of Standards and Technology, Building 225, Room A-323, Gaithersburg, MD 20899; 301-975-2757; or online at http://www.eeel.nist.gov/810.02/index.html

Back to school zits?

No need to go to the prom with pimples. This clearinghouse can provide you with a free information packet called *Acne Information*.

Contact: National Arthritis and Musculoskeletal and Skin Diseases Information Clearinghouse, 1 AMS Way, Bethesda, MD 20892; 301-495-4484; or online at http://www.nih.gov/niams/

Majoring in stress?

The pressure can get to everyone. The National Institute of Mental Health has a publication, *Plain Talk About Stress*, which discusses the three stages of physical and mental stress and how to recognize their symptoms and provides suggestions for dealing with stress. Also available in Spanish.

Contact: Public Inquiries, National Institute of Mental Health, Room 7C-02, 5600 Fishers Lane, Rockville, MD 20892; 301-443-4513; or online at http://www.nimh.nih.gov

What's fair is fair, scientifically speaking

Stumped for a good science project idea? Request a free copy of *Science Fair Projects* which lists references for some interesting projects, including lasers, astronomy, and holograms.

Contact: Science and Technology Division, Library of Congress, Washington, DC 20540; 202-707-5664; or online at http://lcweb.loc.gov

Your neighborhood college

The convenience, services, and cost make community colleges the way to go for many students. The ERIC Clearinghouse for Community Colleges can provide you with a wealth of information regarding 2-year community and junior colleges, technical institutes, and 2-year branch university campuses. They have many publications including these free bibliographies:

• *Job Training in the Community College*

• *Student Personnel in the Community College*

• *Vocational Education in the Community College*

Contact: University of California, Los Angeles, ERIC Clearinghouse for Community Colleges, 3051 Moore Hall, Box 951521, Los Angeles, CA 90095; 310-825-3931, 800-832-8256; or online at http://www.gse.ucla.edu/eric/eric.html

Flight schools

Want to learn how to fly but don't know where to start? The Federal Aviation Administration (FAA) can help you get off the ground, as they have a listing of all the flight schools in the country, including name, address, telephone number, and listing of courses offered.

Write to: Federal Aviation Administration (FAA), Attention: AFS 620, P.O. Box 25082, Oklahoma City, OK 73125; 405-954-4173, Fax: 405-954-4655; or online at http://www.faa.gov

Native American programs

The Bureau of Indian Affairs sponsors several programs to promote higher education for Native Americans. They have the Higher Education Grant Program, Special Higher Education Grant Program, Adult Education Program, Summer Law Program and more. A good source of information on Indian education in general is the free annual *Office of Indian Education Programs Education Directory*.

Contact: Office of Indian Education Programs, Bureau of Indian Affairs, U.S. Department of the Interior, 1849 C Street, NW, Washington, DC 20240; 202-208-4871; or online at http://shaman.unm.edu/oiep/home.htm

Helping those in need

Would you like to help people with disabilities live independently or get a good job? There are special programs where federal money is sent to colleges and universities to help cover scholarships and fellowships for students in the fields of physical medicine and rehabilitation.

To learn what schools received funds and the type of degrees covered, contact: Rehabilitation Services Administration, Office of Developmental Programs, U.S. Department of Education, MES Bldg., Room 2531, 330 C St., SW, Washington, DC 20202; 202-205-5482; or online at http://www.ed.gov/offices/osers/rsa/

College-bound and gagged

Fear of public speaking is nothing to get choked up about. Uncle Sam believes in freedom of speech. The Congressional Research Service has put together several packets of information on speech writing for members of Congress, which you can get for free just by contacting your representative or senators.

The reports cover general public speaking information, and provide ideas for all the major national holidays. Some of the reports include:

• *Public Speaking, Bibliography-in-Brief*

• *Speechwriting and Delivery*, Info Pack

• *Speech Material: Fourth of July,* Info Pack

• *Speech Material: Graduation*, Info Pack

• *Speech Material: Martin Luther King's Birthday*, Info Pack.

Contact: Your Congressman, The Capitol, Washington, DC 20510; 202-224-3121; or online at http://www.senate.gov/ or http://www.house.gov/

CD-ROM vs. floppy disks?

Are you having a hard time trying to decide whether you should buy a CD-ROM or stay with your computer floppy disks? The ERIC Clearinghouse on Information and Technology can send you a number of studies comparing the different types of computer-based media.

Contact: ERIC Clearinghouse on Information and Technology, 4-194 Center for Science Technology, Syracuse, NY 13244-4100; 315-443-3640, 800-464-9107; or online at http://ericir.syr.edu/ithome

I'm studying abroad

Want to be part of an exchange program? The Institute of International Education can provide you with information on public and private organizations which sponsor international exchange activities.

The free brochure *Fulbright Grants and Other Grants for Graduate Study Abroad* contains valuable information both on the Fulbright program and on other organizations sponsoring exchanges.

Contact: Institute of International Education, 809 United Nations Plaza, New York, NY 10017; 212-984-5330; or online at http://www.iie.org

Free engineering degree

Few people know that one way to get an engineering degree—for free —without having to join the military, and without being low-income, is through the Merchant Marine Academy in Kings Point, N.Y. Not only is tuition covered, but so are your books and uniform costs, and you'll receive a monthly stipend for the work you'll be assigned.

Contact: Admissions Officer, U.S. Merchant Marine Academy, Kings Point, N.Y. 11024-1699; 516-773-5391, 800-732-6267 (outside N.Y.); or online at http://www.usmma.edu

Tests: You've got to take them

No matter what you do, you need to take tests—whether it is to get into a college or to keep your GPA high. The question is, can you become a better test-taker? The ERIC Clearinghouse on Assessment and Evaluation has several free two-page information sheets designed to help improve your study and testing habits. You can request:

• *Improving the Quality of Student Notes*

• *Improving Your Test-Taking Skills*

• *Making the A: How to Study for a Test*

To get your copies, contact: Clearinghouse on Assessment and Evaluation, Catholic University of America, Department of Education, O'Boyle Hall, Washington, DC 20064; 800-464-3742; or online at http://ericae2. educ.cua.edu/

Pilot tests

Thinking about taking flying lessons or studying for your pilot's test? Uncle Sam can come to your rescue with several publications to help you along.

- *Guide to Aviation Education Resources* (050-007-01106-7; $2) is a complete list of programs and sources to get you started in aviation.

- *Recreational Pilot Practical Test Standards* (050-007-00827-9; $5.50) establishes the standards for the recreational pilot certification practical tests for airplanes and rotorcraft.

- *Recreational Pilot and Private Pilot Knowledge Test Guide* (050-007-01085-1; $3) describes the knowledge requirements for certification, with sample test questions and procedures.

For your copies contact: Superintendent of Documents, U.S. Government Printing Office, Washington, DC 20402; 202-512-1800; or online at http://www.gpo.gov

Money to become a librarian

Do you want to share your love of books with the world? How about helping people do research using the latest information technologies? You can do all of this with a library degree.

The Library Programs office of the U.S. Department of Education awards funds to colleges and universities, who in turn, pass the money onto students in the form of fellowships or traineeships with stipends.

To learn more about the program, contact: Discretionary Library Programs Division, Library Programs, Office of Educational Research and Improvement, U.S. Department of Education, 555 New Jersey Ave., NW, Washington, DC 20208; 202-606-5551; or online at http://www.ed.gov.

To learn more about accredited library programs which can receive these funds, contact: The American Library Association, Office of Accreditation, 50 E. Huron St., Chicago, IL 60611; 800-545-2433; or online at http://www.ala.org

Crime: Get in on a growth market

To increase the number of persons who are qualified to teach or do research in criminal justice, fellowship opportunities are available to undergraduate and graduate students to visit the National Institute of Justice and work with the staff for 10-16 weeks.

Detailed information on the National Institute of Justice Fellowships can be received by contacting the National Criminal Justice Reference Service, Box 6000, Rockville, MD 20850, 800-851-3420; or online at http://www.ncjrs.org

Volunteer and earn money to pay for school

If you want to save the world and get money for college too, consider AmeriCorps. They'll give you living expenses, health care and child care while you serve a local non-profit organization and they'll throw in $1,000 to $4,725 to help pay for your college or vocational training.

Contact the Corporation for National Service to locate programs in your area. Or, to apply for programs at the national level contact: Corporation for National Service, 1201 New York Ave., NW, Washington, DC 20525; 800-94-ACORPS; or online at http://www.cns.gov

Scholarships if you want to work for Uncle Sam

College juniors interested in careers in public service can get up to $3,000 for their senior year and $27,000 for graduate studies. A faculty representative is appointed for each school and is responsible for soliciting recommendations on students with significant potential for leadership, conducting a competition on campus, and forwarding the institution's official nomination to the Truman Scholarship Review Committee.

For more information, write: Harry S. Truman Scholarship Foundation, 712 Jackson Place, NW, Washington, DC 20006; 202-395-4831; or online at http://www.truman.gov

Scholarships and internships

Millions of dollars are available to students each year in the form of fellowships and scholarships. You just need to know where to look.

The Congressional Research Service (CRS) has put together a publication titled, *Internships and Fellowships* (IP0631) Info Pack which lists information to get you started in your search. You must request this free publication through your congressman.

Contact: Your Congressman, U.S. Capitol, Washington, DC 20510; 202-224-3121; or online at http://www.house.gov or http://www.senate.gov

Money for disadvantaged students to study nursing

If you always wanted to be a nurse, don't let the lack of money stand in your way. Grants have been awarded to institutions to help support nursing students who come from disadvantaged backgrounds. Students must apply to those institutions that received the money.

For a listing of those institutions or more information, contact: U.S. Department of Health and Human Services, U.S. Public Health Service, Health

Resources and Services Administration, Bureau of Health Professions, Division of Student Assistance, 5600 Fishers Lane, Rockville, MD 20857; 301-443-2060; or online at http://www.os.dhhs.gov/about/opdivs/phs.html

Scholarships to those who want to serve the community

Grants are provided to community organizations who in turn offer scholarships to individuals willing to serve that community as physicians, certified nurse practitioners, physician assistants, or certified nurse midwives. A year of service is required for each year of financial assistance.

For information on organizations offering these scholarships contact: National Health Service Corps, Health Resources Development Branch, Public Health Service, 4350 East-West Highway, Rockville, MD 20857; 301-594-4180, 800-221-9393; or online at http://www.bphc.hrsa.dhhs.gov/nhsc/

For your garden

Chapter 7

For your garden

Lawn care do's

Want the best lawn in the neighborhood without having to use every chemical additive known to science? *Healthy Lawn, Healthy Environment*, a free environmental fact sheet, lists the do's and don'ts to help you on your way to a healthy, safe, attractive lawn.

Contact: National Center for Environmental Publications and Information, P.O. Box 42419, Cincinnati, OH 45242; 800-490-9198; or online at http://www.epa.gov

Don't move gypsy moth

Gypsy moths have defoliated up to 13 million acres of trees in one season, so now there is a regulation intended to prevent the interstate spread of this pest. How do you know if you have gypsy moth problems in your area, or what you can do to eradicate this pest which does not have many natural enemies?

Don't Move Gypsy Moth is a free publication which describes the various stages in the life of a gypsy moth, what to look for, and how to prevent their spreading into other neighborhoods.

Contact: Animal and Plant Health Inspection Service, U.S. Department of Agriculture, 4700 River Road, Riverdale, MD 20737; 301-734-5524; or online at http://www.aphis.usda.gov

Your garden hotline

Tired of your plants dying year after year? Just take a minute to talk to the horticulture experts at your local Cooperative Extension Service offices.

Almost all Extension Services operate a special gardening hotline to answer all of your plant questions. They can provide diagnoses and even offer some remedies that just may save your yard.

Look in the blue pages of your phone book for the office nearest you, or for help in finding the correct office, contact: Cooperative State Research Education and Extension Service, U.S. Department of Agriculture, Room 3328, Washington, DC 20250; 202-720-3029; or online at http://www.reeusda.gov

A rose by your own name?

What do *Donna Darlin, Twocherish*, and *George Vancouver* have in common? They're all names of roses chosen by the owners of their patents.

United States patent law provides for the granting of a patent to anyone who has invented or discovered and asexually reproduced any distinct and new variety of plant, including cultivated sports, mutants, hybrids, and newly found seedlings, other than a tuber-propagated plant or a plant found in an uncultivated state.

Want more information on obtaining a patent, or searching existing patents? Contact: United States Patent and Trademark Office, Washington, DC 20231; 800-703-4357; or online at http://www.uspto.gov

Plant facts

How deep do I plant Bermuda grass? Who sells Scarlet Globemallow in my part of the country?

The Plant Materials Program of the Natural Resources Conservation Service develops plant materials and plant technology for the conservation of our nation's natural resources.

Among their publications are:

• *Fact Sheets*—for information about a conservation plant.

• *Sources of Plant Materials*—look here for seed and plant sources around the country.

Contact: National Resources Conservation Service, U.S. Department of Agriculture, P.O. Box 2890, Washington, DC 20013; 202-720-3210; or online at http://www.nrcs.usda.gov/

Work the soil

Soil surveys are used not only for conservation purposes, but also to identify suitable lands for a wide variety of uses, from maintaining crops to urban uses.

Get the scoop on your dirt through some of the free publications available from the Natural Resources Conservation Service. The titles include:

• *In Partnership with People and a Healthy Land*

Contact: Natural Resources Conservation Service, U.S. Department of Agriculture, P.O. Box 2890, Washington, DC 20013; 202-720-3210; or online at http://www.nrcs.usda.gov/

The dirt people

Find out the latest information by going to the source, the U.S. Department of Agriculture (USDA) that is. You can get the *Agriculture Fact Book* ($14) which is published annually and details the mission of the many USDA agencies and provides a plethora of information about agriculture in the United States.

For your copy contact: Superintendent of Documents, U.S. Government Printing Office, Washington, DC 20402; 202-512-1800; or online at http://www.gpo.gov

Dig in

Want to grow your own herbs? What about roses?

If you need more information on some gardening projects, request one of the free reference guides available from the Science and Technology division under the general title, *LC Science Tracer Bullet*.

These guides are designed to help readers locate published material on subjects about which they have only general knowledge. The following is a list of Tracer Bullets dealing with gardening:

- 91-8 *Medicinal Plants*

- 94-5 *Pesticides and Foods*

- 90-4 *Poisonous Plants*

- 96-1 *Edible Wild Plants*

- 88-5 *Soil Erosion*

Contact: Science and Technology Division, Reference Section, Library of Congress, Washington, DC 20540; 202-707-5580; or online at http://lcweb2.loc.gov/sctb/

For your grand-parents

Chapter 8

For your grandparents

Jog the dog

Studies show seniors well into their seventies can benefit from regular exercise, especially lifting weights. Women who pump iron can greatly reduce their risk of osteoporosis, and take care of unwanted overtures from amorous geezers. The National Institute on Aging has an "Exercise Packet" containing articles and other helpful information on the benefits of exercise.

Contact: National Institute on Aging, The Information Center, P.O. Box 8057 - Exercise, Gaithersburg, MD 20898; 800-222-2225; or online at http://www.nih.gov/nia

One depression was enough

Don't let life's roller coaster put you in the dumps. A good attitude is a priceless accomplishment and there are plenty of teachers out there for when you feel lonely or blue. You can get several publications on depression including the free booklet, *If You're Over 65 and Feeling Depressed...Treatment Brings New Hope* which outlines the signs and symptoms of this condition.

Contact: National Institute of Mental Health, 5600 Fishers Lane, Room 7C02, Rockville, MD 20857; 301-443-4513; or online at http://www.nimh.nih.gov/newdart/over65.htm

Over the rainbow coalition

Ellis Island and the Statue of Liberty represent Oz and the Wizard for millions of immigrants following the yellow brick road to freedom. And yes, Dorothy, many eventually made it to Kansas.

More than 12 million immigrants passed through Ellis Island on their search for freedom. For a free Statue of Liberty pamphlet and a booklet entitled *Ellis Island and Statue of Liberty* describing the importance of these historical sites, contact: Office of Public Inquiries, National Park Service, P.O. Box 37127, Washington, DC 20013-7127; 202-208-4747; or online at http://www.nps.gov

No more forget-me-knots

Tying a piece of string around the finger isn't going to help. Neither is accepting memory loss as a simple fact of aging. Plenty of conditions cause forgetfulness, including stress.

A free Age Page publication called *Forgetfulness in Old Age: It's Not What You Think* is available from National Institute on Aging, Information Center, P.O. Box 8057, Gaithersburg, MD 20898; 800-222-2225; or online at http://www.nih.gov/nia

Retirement travel made easy

Now that you have time to travel, you better hit the open road. Visit those historic sites you read about long ago or fish in some of the wildlife refuges.

Administered by the federal government, the Golden Age Passport is a lifetime entrance pass to national parks, monuments, historic sites, recreation areas and national wildlife refuges which charge entrance fees.

It is issued to citizens or permanent residents of the U.S. who are 62 or older. It also provides a 50% discount on federal use fees charged for facilities and services such as camping, boat launching, parking, and more.

For application information request the free brochure *Federal Recreation Passport Program* from National Park Service, Office of Public Inquiries, U.S. Department of the Interior, P.O. Box 37127, Washington, DC 20013; 202-208-4747; or online at http://www.nps.gov

Make their 80th special

Anyone who lives to be 80 deserves something special. The president will send a special birthday greeting to anyone 80 or over.

All you need to do is send in a special request to The White House Greetings Office, Room 91, 1600 Pennsylvania Ave., NW, Washington, DC 20500.

Senior citizen c-sections?

Cataract surgery has become so common among senior Americans that someone investigated it (and it wasn't 20/20). Guess what they found? Many are unnecessary.

To help you and your doctor decide what is best for you, ask for a free copy of the patient and physician guidelines for cataract surgery titled *Cataract In Adults* from: Agency for Health Care Policy and Research, Publications Clearinghouse, P.O. Box 8547, Silver Spring, MD 20907; 800-358-9295; or online at http://www.ahcpr.gov

Hearing is believing

There are hearing aids for all types of hearing impairments which is why it is important to learn all you can before making a decision, especially since the Food and Drug Administration required six hearing aid manufacturers to adjust their ads due to incorrect advertising.

For information on hearing and hearing aids and a copy of the free publication *Deafness, Hearing, and Hearing Disorders Information Resources for Consumers*, contact: National Institute on Deafness and Other Communication Disorders Clearinghouse, 1 Communication Avenue, Bethesda, MD 20892-3456; 800-241-1044, 800-241-1055 (TDD); or online at http://www.nih.gov/nidcd/

The downside of longevity

Live long enough and you might forget your problems, and just about everything else, too. Uncle Sam has set up an entire medical center devoted to tracking the latest in Alzheimer's research and where to go for the best care and treatment.

They have many free publications including *Alzheimer's Disease: A Caregiver and Patient Resource List* and *Talking With Your Doctor: A Guide for Older People.*

Contact: Alzheimer's Disease Education and Referral Center, P.O. Box 8250, Silver Spring, MD 20907; 800-438-4380; or online at http://www.alzheimers.org/

Smoke signals

Why kick cigarettes late in life? If you've been smoking for years, the damage has already been done, right? Wrong.

The latest studies show that even after years of tar and nicotine, smokers who quit live longer, healthier, happier lives.

Get a copy of *Good News For Smokers Over 50* from Office on Smoking and Health, Centers for Disease Control, 4770 Buford Highway, NE, MS K-50, Atlanta, GA 30341-3724; 800-232-1311; or online at http://www.cdc.gov/nccdphp/osh/

Should my diet change as I get older?

Should I change my diet now that I'm older? You hear so much about salt intake, should I lower mine? The National Institute on Aging can answer these questions and more. The Institute makes available for free several "Age Pages" which offer tips for senior citizens. Those dealing with nutrition include:

- *Be Sensible About Salt*—discusses the reduction of salt.

- *Constipation*—explains cause and treatment of constipation.

- *Dealing with Diabetes*—explains detection, symptoms, and treatment of diabetes.

- *Dietary Supplements: More Is Not Always Better*—discusses the pros and cons of taking vitamins and minerals.

- *Digestive Do's and Don'ts*—shows steps necessary to keep your digestive system working at its best.

- *Don't Take It Easy—Exercise!*—shows how to design and find an exercise program.

- *Hints For Shopping, Cooking, and Enjoying Meals*—gives shopping and cooking tips.

• *Nutrition: A Lifelong Concern*—explains the major nutrition groups and how to get them into your diet.

Contact: National Institute on Aging, P.O. Box 8057, Gaithersburg, MD 20898; 800-222-2225; or online at http://www.nih.gov/nia

Your ship has come in

If your mom, dad, or grandparents always talk about their Navy stint, you can really bring it back to life with some help from the Cartographic and Architectural Branch of the National Archives. This office compiles the plans of all Navy ships since the Navy was founded. For a copy of a ship plan you must make your request in writing, and provide ship name and designation. The National Archives now uses vendors for all reproduction services. For a list of vendors and prices, call 301-713-7030. You can also fax your request to 301-713-7488.

For more information contact: Cartographic and Architectural Branch, National Archives and Records Administration, 8601 Adelphi Rd., College Park, MD 20740-6001; 301-713-7040; or online at http://www.nara.gov/

Grandma getting a little shorter?

Bone loss and brittle bones affect as many as 24 million Americans in the form of osteoporosis. Getting enough calcium and maintaining a good exercise program are two steps you can take to help prevent osteoporosis.

To learn more about the causes, risk factors, and treatment, contact: Osteoporosis and Related Bone Diseases National Resource Center, 1150 17th St., NW, Suite 500, Washington, DC 20036; 800-624-BONE; or online at http://www.osteo.org/

Stronger medicine

A medicine cabinet full of prescription drugs is an accident waiting to happen. Many elderly patients are forgetful or distracted and drugs in the wrong combination can be fatal.

Out-of-date medications won't control life-threatening conditions such as hypertension or diabetes. The government can tell you how to get organized through a series of free articles called *How To Take Your Medicines.*

Contact: Office of Consumer Affairs, Food and Drug Administration, 5600 Fishers Lane, HFE-88, Rockville, MD 20857; 800-532-4440, 301-443-3170; or online at http://www.fda.gov/

A special 50th wedding anniversary

You can request a special anniversary greeting from the president for your parents' or grandparents' 50th anniversary.

All it takes is a written request to the White House Greetings Office, Room 91, 1600 Pennsylvania Ave., NW, Washington, DC 20500.

Your grandparents' boat

Did your grandparents come to the country by boat? The National Archives maintains ship passenger arrival records dating from 1820 for most east and gulf coast ports, a few lists dating from 1800 for Philadelphia, and from the 1890's for San Francisco and Seattle. Archives staff can conduct free searches if you know the full name of the passenger, the port of entry, and the approximate date of arrival. If they find your grandparents' name, you can purchase a copy of the log for only $10.

For more information contact: Reference Services Branch, National Archives and Records Administration, 8th St. and Pennsylvania Ave., NW, Washington, DC 20408; 202-501-5400.

When it is time to move

Selecting a nursing home is one of the most important and difficult decisions that you may be asked to make—either for yourself or for a member of your family. A free publication, *Guide to Choosing a Nursing Home*, provides information on questions you should ask, payment information, as well as a checklist of things you should look for when visiting a facility.

For your copy write to: Health Care Financing Administration, U.S. Department of Health and Human Services, 6325 Security Blvd., Baltimore, MD 21244; 410-786-3000; or online at http://www.hcfa.gov/

World War II memorabilia

If one of your loved ones is a WWII veteran or even a history buff, the Archives has a picture for you.

The Second World War was documented on a huge scale by thousands of photographers who created millions of pictures.

Every activity of the war was depicted—training, combat, support services, and more. A free catalogue is available which lists photographs by subject and campaign. Prices start at $6 for an 8 x 10.

For more information contact: Still Picture Branch, National Archives, 8601 Adelphi Rd., College Park, MD 20740; 301-713-6625 ext. 221.

Uncle Sam is hiring 55 and up

The U.S. Department of Labor's Senior Community Service Employment Program promotes the creation of part time jobs in community service activities for jobless, low-income persons who are at least 55 years old and have poor employment prospects. Individuals work in part time jobs at senior citizens' centers, schools, or hospitals, programs for the handicapped, and beautification and restoration projects.

Contact your state office for the aging, area agencies on aging or the Older Workers Program, U.S. Department of Labor, Employment and Training Administration, 200 Constitution Ave., NW, Room C4524, Washington, DC 20210; 202-219-4778; or online at http://www.doleta.gov

Service hotline for the elderly

The Eldercare Locator is a nationwide service designed to help people find information about community services for older people.

Call between 9 am and 11 pm (EST), and you'll be put in touch with thousands of state and local resources on everything from finding them help, health care, social services, guardianship, and much more.

Contact: Eldercare Locator, Administration on Aging, 330 Independence Ave., SW, Room 4656, Washington, DC 20201; 800-677-1116; or online at http://www.ageinfo.org/elderloc/elderloc.html

Medicare made easy

It is difficult enough trying to figure out all the doctor bills and insurance forms. What does Medicare cover? Should you get a Medigap policy? What if you have a problem with Medicare paying a claim? The Health Care Financing Administration has put together several free publications which can answer these questions and more. Some of the titles include:

- *Medicare Handbook*

- *Guide to Health Insurance For People With Medicare*

- *Medicare and Home Health Care*

- *Medicare and Your Physician's Bill*

- *Savings for Qualified Beneficiaries*

You can request these publications and more by calling Medicare Hotline, Health Care Financing Administration, U.S. Department of Health and Human Services, 6325 Security Blvd., Baltimore, MD 21244; 800-638-6833; or online at http://www.hcfa.gov/medicare/medicare.htm

Share a little love

The Foster Grandparent Program offers volunteer opportunities to low-income persons 60 and older to provide one-to-one assistance to children with special and exceptional needs.

Volunteers help infants abandoned at birth, addicted to drugs, HIV-positive, and children and teens who are struggling. Applicants must be willing to serve 20 hours per week. Volunteers work in areas such as Head Start projects, hospitals, public schools, day care centers, and juvenile detention centers. Volunteers receive a modest tax-free allowance or stipend.

Contact: Foster Grandparent Program, Corporation For National Service, 1201 New York Ave., NW, Washington, DC 20525; 800-942-2677; or online at http://www.cns.gov/senior/sc_fgp.html

Funds for your retirement

Concerned about your retirement because your company pension is shaky? Or does it just seem like you're not getting everything out of your pension that you should?

The Special Committee on Aging of the United States Senate has compiled a number of useful publications for seniors, including *Shortchanged: Pension Miscalculations* (#105-06). The Committee will also investigate selected reports of fraud involving seniors.

Contact Senate Special Committee on Aging, G31 Dirksen Senate Bldg., Washington, DC 20510; 202-224-5364; or online at http://www.senate.gov/~aging/

For your health

Chapter 9

For your health

What your children should know

AIDS Prevention Guide is written for parents and other adults concerned about young people. It provides ideas to help adults start a conversation about AIDS.

It presents the facts about AIDS, geared to elementary and junior and senior high school students, and offers common questions and accurate answers. It includes handouts for young people aged 10 to 20 years.

Contact: CDC National AIDS Information Clearinghouse, P.O. Box 6003, Rockville, MD 20850; 800-458-5231; or online at http://www.cdcnac.org/

Don't run with scissors

Want to know how many children under the age of five are injured while playing with toys? Want to learn about the safety of all-terrain vehicles?

The National Injury Information Clearinghouse maintains a database of detailed investigative reports of injuries associated with consumer products. You can find the victim's background, including age, race, injury diagnosis, consumer product involved, and more. The Clearinghouse distributes documents and will fulfill search requests usually at no charge.

Contact: National Injury Information Clearinghouse, U.S. Consumer Product Safety Commission, 4330 East-West Highway, Washington, DC 20207; 301-504-0424, 800-638-2772; or online at http://www.cpsc.gov

You can cure a cold with chicken soup

Before grandma makes you take another spoonful, check out the facts with the Food and Drug Administration (FDA). There have been no studies done on the benefits of chicken soup, but common sense says that nutritious fluids and rest will help you recuperate.

An FDA consumer article, *What to Do for Colds and Flu*, explains the difference between colds and flu, discusses the pros and cons of flu shots, and describes the different types of cold remedies available.

For your free copy contact: Food and Drug Administration, Office of Consumer Affairs (HFE-88), 5600 Fishers Lane, Rockville, MD 20857; 301-443-3170, 800-532-4440; or online at http://www.fda.gov/

Caring for children with AIDS

AIDS is a scary topic, especially when it affects children. The National Maternal and Child Health Clearinghouse has several free publications concerned with AIDS and children.

Some of the titles include:

- *Pregnancy and HIV: Is AZT the Right Choice for You and Your Baby?*

- *Making Connections: Building Family Support Networks for Families Living with HIV*

- *A Guide: Family-Centered Comprehensive Care for Children with HIV Infection*

Contact: National Maternal and Child Health Clearinghouse, 2070 Chainbridge Rd., Suite 450, Vienna, VA 22182-2536; 703-356-1964.

Poisoning—number one preventable childhood disease

Childhood lead poisoning is one of the most common pediatric health problems in the United States today, and it is entirely preventable. New data indicate significant adverse effects of lead exposure in children at blood lead levels previously believed to be safe. For more information on lead poisoning, and a free copy of the *Centers for Disease Control's (CDC) Preventing Lead Poisoning in Young Children,* contact the office listed below.

Contact: Lead Poisoning Prevention Branch, National Center for Environmental Health, Centers for Disease Control (CDC), 4770 Buford Highway, NE, F-42, Atlanta, GA 30341; 770-488-7330; or online at:

http://www.cdc.gov/nceh/programs/lead/lead.htm

Help for handicapped and gifted children

ERIC (Educational Resources Information Center) Clearinghouse on Disabilities and Gifted Education gathers and disseminates educational information on disabilities and giftedness across all age-levels.

They have:

- publications

- digests (2-4 page summaries of current topics),

- research briefs

- issue briefs

- directories of currently funded research

- topical info packets and flyer files

- catalog of products and services available to the special educator

They also have database searches and reprints. Two free digests available include *Effective Practices for Preparing Young Children with Disabilities for School*, which explains early intervention services, and *Educating Exceptional Children* which explains some of the terminology and trends.

Contact: ERIC Clearinghouse on Disabilities and Gifted Education, Council for Exceptional Children, 1920 Association Dr., Reston, VA 22091; 703-264-9474, 800-328-0272; or online at http://www.cec.sped.org/er_menu.htm

Down syndrome, mental retardation, and learning disabilities

The National Institute of Child Health and Human Development conducts and supports research on the reproductive, developmental, and behavioral processes that determine the health of children, adults, families, and populations.

Research for mothers, children, and families is designed to advance knowledge of fetal development, pregnancy, and birth and to contribute to the prevention and treatment of mental retardation.

Some of the publications include:

- *Facts About Down Syndrome*

- *Facts About Dyslexia*

- *Learning Disabilities: A Report to the U.S. Congress*

Contact: National Institute of Child Health and Human Development, National Institutes of Health, Building 31, Room 2A32, 9000 Rockville Pike, Bethesda, MD 20892; 301-496-5133; or online at http://www.nih.gov/nichd/

Help for those helping low-income mothers

Healthy Mothers, Healthy Babies—A Compendium of Program Ideas for Servicing Low-Income Women provides useful suggestions to health care providers and children who work with low income populations, and suggests program planning and policy directions for state and national organizations concerned with maternal and infant health.

Contact: National Clearinghouse for Primary Care Information, 2070 Chain Bridge Rd., Vienna, VA 22182; 800-400-2742; or online at http://158.72.85.159/ncpci/

Children and mental health

The National Institute of Mental Health (NIMH) conducts research on depression and other mental disorders, distributes information, and conducts demonstration programs for the prevention, treatment, and rehabilitation of the mentally ill.

NIMH has several publications which deal with mental health in children. These publications are available at no charge.

Titles include:

• *Plain Talk About Dealing With the Angry Child*

• *Plain Talk About Raising Children*

• *Plain Talk About Adolescence*

Contact: National Institute of Mental Health, 5600 Fishers Lane, Room 7C02, Rockville, MD 20892; 301-443-4513; or online at http://www.nimh.nih.gov/

Sudden Infant Death hotline

The National Sudden Infant Death Syndrome Resource Center was established to provide information and educational materials on Sudden Infant Death Syndrome (SIDS), apnea, and other related issues. The staff responds to information requests from professionals, families with SIDS-related deaths, and the general public by sending written materials and making referrals.

The Center maintains a library of reference materials and mailing lists of state programs, groups, and individuals concerned with SIDS. Their publications include bibliographies on SIDS and self-help support groups, a publications catalogue, and a newsletter.

Some of their free publications include:

• *What is SIDS?*

• *Sudden Infant Death: Some Facts You Should Know*

National Sudden Infant Death Syndrome Resource Center, 2070 Chain Bridge Rd., Suite 450, Vienna, VA 22182; 703-821-8955; or online at http://www.circsol.com/sids/

Programs for children of alcoholics

The Clearinghouse for Alcohol and Drug Information has a wealth of information regarding children of alcoholics.

Risk and Reality: Teaching Pre-school Children Affected by Substance Abuse includes a 30-minute videotape, a teacher's guide, and a research review that identifies specific techniques teachers can use when working with these children ($12.50).

Teaching Children Affected by Substance Abuse is a 30-minute videotape and teacher's guide for elementary school staff who work with children exposed to substance abuse ($12.50).

Contact: National Clearinghouse for Alcohol and Drug Information, P.O. Box 2345, Rockville, MD 20847; 800-729-6686; or online at http://www.health.org

Parent guides for alcohol and drug information

Are you concerned that your child may have a problem with alcohol or drugs? Do you want to know what signs to look for?

The National Clearinghouse for Drug and Alcohol Information can help and has the following free publications available, dealing with drug and alcohol use:

- *How Not to Get High, Get Stupid, Get AIDS: A Guide to Partying.*

- *A Guide for Teens: Does Your Friend Have an Alcohol or Other Drug Problem? What You Can Do to Help.*

- *How Getting High Can Get You AIDS.*

- *If You Drink Too Much Beer...You Drink Too Much.*

- *Teen Drinking Prevention Program.*

- *Alcohol...We're Not Buying It* (Poster).

- *Tips for Teens About Marijuana.*

• *If You Change Your Mind Student Magazine.*

• *Straight At Ya* (video; $12.50)

• *Fast Forward Future* (video; $12.50)

Contact: National Clearinghouse for Alcohol and Drug Information, P.O. Box 2345, Rockville, MD 20847; 800-729-6686; or online at http://www.health.org

Call for the answer. . . the Smoking Hotline

The Smoking Hotline can answer all your questions regarding cigarettes and stop smoking methods.

It can provide fact sheets, pamphlets, posters and other publications, as well as information in response to inquiries.

The Center can access information on the Combined Health Information Database, and its library and reading room are open to the public.

Some of the free publications they have include:

• *Don't Let Another Year Go Up In Smoke*—tips to help you stop smoking.

• *Out of the Ashes: Choosing a Method To Quit Smoking*—outlines various methods of quitting.

• *Office on Smoking and Health's Information Resources*—outlines local and community resources.

• *Tobacco Control Information Sources*—a listing of government agencies and nonprofit organizations that provide information about smoking and health.

Contact: Office on Smoking and Health, Centers for Disease Control, 4770 Buford Hwy., Mail Stop K-50, Atlanta, GA 30341-3724; 800-CDC-1311; or online at http://www.cdc.gov/tobacco

Think you can't get pregnant because you have endometriosis?

Think again! While the pregnancy rates for women with endometriosis remain lower than those of the general population, most women with this condition do not experience fertility problems.

It is estimated that between 10 and 20 percent of American women of childbearing age have endometriosis. The National Institute of Child Health and Human Development conducts research to develop an optimal treatment for endometriosis.

For a free booklet, *Facts About Endometriosis*, or for information on current research or other organizations for further assistance, contact: The National Institute of Child Health and Human Development, National Institutes of Health, Bldg. 31, Room 2A32, Bethesda, MD 20892; 301-496-5133; or online at http://www.nih.gov/nichd

Parents of disabled children are not alone

The National Information Center for Children and Youth with Disabilities helps parents of handicapped children and disabled adults locate services and parent support groups, focusing on the needs of rural areas, culturally diverse populations, and severely handicapped people. This center also provides information on vocational/transitional issues, special education, and legal rights and advocacy.

It provides fact sheets on specific disabilities, including autism, cerebral palsy, hearing impairments, Down syndrome, epilepsy, learning disabilities, mental retardation, physical disabilities, speech and language impairments, spina bifida, and visual impairments.

The materials designed especially for parents include:

- *Parents' Guide to Accessing Programs for Infants, Toddlers, Preschoolers with Disabilities* (ages 0-5)

- *Parents' Guide to Accessing Parent Groups*

- *A Parent's Guide: Accessing the ERIC Resource Collection*

- *A Parent's Guide to Doctors, Disabilities, and the Family*

- *A Parent's Guide: Planning a Move; Mapping Your Strategy*

- *A Parent's Guide: Special Education and Related Services: Communicating Through Letter Writing*

Contact: National Information Center for Children and Youth with Disabilities, P.O. Box 1492, Washington, DC 20013; 800-695-0285; or online at http://www.nichcy.org

Does your child have asthma?

The Asthma Clearinghouse is a new clearinghouse, providing publications, reports, resources, and referrals to experts in the field of asthma. One report, the *Expert Panel Report: Guidelines for the Diagnosis and Management of Asthma*, explains the diagnosis, therapy, and other considerations for those that suffer from asthma. Asthma Education Materials and Resources lists sources of information for patients and their families.

The Clearinghouse can answer your questions or can direct you to those who can. For more information, contact: National Asthma Education and Prevention Program, 7200 Wisconsin Ave., P.O. Box 30105, Bethesda, MD 20824; 301-251-1222; or online at http://www.nhlbi.nih.gov/

Mental health and you

Are you feeling troubled and looking for help? There seem to be more types of therapy than there are breakfast cereals. How do you know what to choose or even look for?

The Consumers Guide to Mental Health Services is a free booklet which explains the different types of services available, questions you should ask, and more.

Contact: National Institute of Mental Health, 5600 Fishers Lane, Room 7C02, Rockville, MD 20892; 301-443-4513; or online at http://www.nimh.nih/gov

A wealth of family planning information

The Office of Population Affairs Clearinghouse provides information on family planning, adolescent pregnancy, and adoption.

The primary audience consists of federally supported service agencies, but it also provides information to family planning service providers, educators, trainers, and consumers throughout the U.S.

A free publications list is available which includes:

- *Information for Men—Your Sterilization Operation*

- *Information for Women—Your Sterilization Operation*

- *Many Teens are Saying "NO"*

- *Family and Adolescent Pregnancy*

- *Your Contraceptive Choices: For Now, For Later*

- *Sexually Transmitted Diseases Treatment Guidelines*

Contact: Office of Population Affairs Clearinghouse, P.O. Box 30686, Bethesda, MD 20824; 301-654-6190; or online at http://www.dhhs.gov/progorg/opa/clearing.html

Special health care needs

Parents whose children have special health care needs are often overwhelmed and isolated because of their child's condition. But help is just a phone call away. The Clearinghouse has an extensive list of free publications concerned with children with special health care needs.

Two helpful publications are *Essential Allies: Families as Advisors*, and *Family/Professional Collaboration for Children with Special Health Needs*.

Contact: National Maternal and Child Health Clearinghouse, 2070 Chain Bridge Rd., Vienna, VA 22182-2536; 703-356-1964; or online at http://www. circsol.com/mch/

Illegal drug use in youth

The Coordinating Council is a group of 16 Federal agencies who held a workshop to develop interagency initiatives to combat the juvenile drug problem.

They produced *Juvenile Alcohol and Other Drug Abuse: A Guide to Federal Initiatives for Prevention, Treatment, and Control* which will serve as a resource for state, local, and private agencies and individuals working to combat juvenile drug and alcohol abuse.

Contact: Office of Juvenile Justice and Delinquency Clearinghouse, P. O. Box 6000, Rockville, MD 20850; 800-638-8736; or online at http://www.ncjrs.org/txtfiles/council.txt

It is estimated that 3 percent to 5 percent of children are affected. The National Institute of Mental Health has a brochure titled *Learning Disabilities*, which discusses ADD and other learning disabilities, as well as providing addresses and phone numbers to other resources and organizations. For your copy contact: National Institute of Mental Health, 5600 Fishers Lane, Room 7C-02, Rockville, MD 20892; 301-443-4513; or online at http://www.nimh. nih.gov/

Clearinghouse on disability information

Wondering if your company complies with the American Disabilities Act? What about trying to find programs to help you?

The Clearinghouse responds to inquiries on a wide range of topics. You can find out about programs serving individuals with disabilities, federal legislation, and federal funding for special programs.

Two free publications to get you on your way include:

- *General Information About Disabilities*— gives an overview of the 13 disabilities defined by the Individuals with Disabilities Education Act.

- *Resources for Adults with Disabilities*—($2) provides resources to help adults with disabilities identify organizations and agencies designed to assist with their specific concerns and needs.

Contact: National Information Center for Children and Youth with Disabilities, P.O. Box 1492, Washington, DC 20013; 800-695-0285; or online at http://www.nichcy.org

Cerebral Palsy in children

The National Institute of Neurological Disorders and Stroke has information about the latest developments on this disorder as well as a free 26-page pamphlet titled *Cerebral Palsy: Hope Through Research*.

They also can provide you with articles, a bibliography, and other resources on this topic.

Contact: National Institute of Neurological Disorders and Stroke, P.O. Box 5801, Bethesda, MD 20824; 800-352-9424; or online at http://www.ninds. nih.gov/

Want to live forever?

Every day the newspaper seems to have a story about a new study or drug that promises great steps forward in the war on aging. Where can you find an objective review of recent findings?

The National Institute on Aging has published a free booklet entitled: *In Search of the Secrets of Aging*. This booklet looks at the current state of knowledge about longevity, theories of aging, the link between genes and life span, the biochemistry of aging, and physiologic clues about the aging process.

Contact the National Institute on Aging, Building 31, Room 5C27, 31 Center Drive, MSC 2292, Bethesda, MD 20892-2292; 800-222-2225; or online at http://www.nih.gov/nia

Second surgical opinion line

Just maybe you don't need a hysterectomy or your gall bladder removed. If you are on Medicare or Medicaid, you can get help finding a physician to give you a second opinion. Keep in mind that studies now show that 30% of all operations are not necessary.

Contact: Health Care Financing Administration, 6325 Security Boulevard, Baltimore, MD 21207, 800-638-6833; or online at http://www.hcfa.gov/

The pain people

Find out whether the pain is of the acute or chronic variety, and then get some helpful suggestions on pain reducing strategies.

The National Institute of Neurological Disorders and Stroke has a free publication, *Chronic Pain: Hope Through Research* which describes causes, research, and treatment of pain, as well as where to go for more help and information.

Contact: National Institute of Neurological Disorders and Stroke, P.O. Box 5801, Bethesda, MD 20824; 800-352-9424; or online at http://www.ninds.nih.gov/

Directory for women's health problems

Who, What, Where: Resources For Women's Health and Aging is a free directory listing resources for women on a variety of topics including menopause, finances, housing options, research, organizations and more. It is a wonderful starting place for gathering information.

Contact: National Institute on Aging, Building 31, Room 5C27, 31 Center Drive, Bethesda, MD 20892; 800-222-2225; or online at http://www.nih.gov/nia/

For your hobbies

10

Chapter 10

For your hobbies

Going fishing without mosquitoes

A slow day at the fishing hole can lead to lots of ribbing. Take the easy way out and stop at the fish store on the way home, but make sure you keep the fish you buy safe to eat.

The Office of Seafood at the Food and Drug Administration has an automated telephone system which can answer your questions regarding seafood storage, cooking, safety, handling, labeling or any problems you may have concerning seafood. Some of the publications include:

- *If You Eat Raw Oysters*

- *Critical Steps for Safer Seafood*

- *Is Something Fishy Going On?*

- *Seafood Safety*

- *Handbook for Requesting Information From the FDA*

For your free publications, or for more information, contact: Seafood Hotline; 800-FDA-4010; or online at http://www.fda.gov

Do you know someone who is a gold digger?

The U.S. Geological Survey distributes a free booklet, *How To Mine and Prospect For Gold*, which can get your gold digger started on the right path.

For a free copy contact: U.S. Geological Survey Information Services, Box 25286, Denver Federal Center, Denver, CO 80225; 303-202-4700; or online at http://www.usgs.org/

Borrow the battle

The photography library of the U.S. Park Service will lend you pictures and slides of national parks, monuments, and battlefields. A great resource for Civil War buffs.

Contact: Photo Library, Office of Public Affairs, National Park Service, U.S. Department of Interior, 18th and C Sts., NW, Washington, DC 20240; 202-208-4997; or online at http://www.nps.gov

A thousand words

If you need to illuminate a talk or presentation, the National Gallery has a lending library of 50,000 images. There's no catalog, so start a wish list. The images can be borrowed through inter-library loan.

For subject specific catalogs or more information contact: National Gallery of Art, Slide Library, Constitution and 6th St., NW, Washington, DC 20565; 202-842-6099; or online at http://www.nga.gov/

For the would-be wine connoisseur

What exactly does all the writing on a wine bottle mean? *What You Should Know About Grape Wine Labels* is a free brochure which describes the elements written on a label for grape wine and what can be learned from the label.

These include brand, vintage date, variety designations, alcohol content, appellation of origin, viticultural area, name or trade name, and estate bottled. These things are very important in choosing a good bottle of wine, so study hard.

Contact: Distribution Center, Bureau of Alcohol, Tobacco, and Firearms, U.S. Department of Treasury, 7943 Angus Court, Springfield, VA 22153; 703-455-7801; or online at http://www.atf.treas.gov/

The wild, wild West

The Bureau of Land Management rides herd on over 270 million acres of range and has the photos to prove it. It also has hundreds of pictures of cowpokes, prospectors and crusty miners.

No catalog is available, but you can request a loan. Include type of photo, time period, or location in your request.

Contact: National Applied Resource Sciences Center (NARSC), P.O. Box 25047, Denver Federal Center, Bldg. 50, Denver, CO 80225-0047; 303-236-2772; or online at http://www.blm.gov/narsc/

Gold rush

Mining for gold did not end in the 1800's, but continues today. Turn your vacation into a true treasure hunt with the help of some free publications available through the U.S. Geological Survey. *Gold* discusses the nature of gold, and the geologic environments in which it is found.

Prospecting for Gold in the United States describes various kinds of gold deposits and their locations. *Suggestions for Prospecting* compares modern prospecting techniques with those of earlier years.

Write your request for these publications to U.S. Geological Survey, Map Distribution, Box 25286, Denver, CO 80225; 800-USA-MAPS; or online at http://www.usgs.gov

Stamp it!

Did the Elvis stamp craze pique your interest? Stamp collecting is the most popular hobby in the world, so join in. The U.S. Postal Service has a pamphlet, *Introduction to Stamp Collecting* (pub. 225), which can help get you on your way to the philatelic hall of fame.

This free publication is available at your local post office or by writing U.S. Postal Service, 475 L'Enfant Plaza West, SW, Washington, DC 20260; or online at http://www.usps.gov

What's this?

Get your kids interested in the outdoors by helping them start a rock collection.

Collecting Rocks is a free publication of the U.S. Geological Survey which describes the origin of major rock types and provides suggestions for starting a rock collection and identifying specimens.

Write for your copy to U.S. Geological Survey, Map Distribution, Box 25286, Denver, CO 80225; 800-USA-MAPS; or online at http://www.usgs.gov

An armchair walk in the woods... and time

The U.S. Forest Service has two entire libraries of photographs and slides dating back to 1890. Topics covered include forestry, timber industry, fish and wildlife, and more.

The Historical Library has images from 1890-1954, with half of the collection on a laser disk. The Current Library can put together photographs or slides based upon your request.

For more ordering or borrowing information contact: Historical Photographs, National Agricultural Library, 10301 Baltimore Blvd., Beltsville, MD 20705; 301-504-5876. Current Library, Forest Service, Office of Public Affairs, U.S. Department of Agriculture, 201 14th St., SW, Washington, DC 20250; 202-205-1760; or online at http://www.fs.fed.us/

Socks included

Free photos of the First Family are available. You can get one with or without Hillary, even an 8x10 of First Feline, "Socks," without any of them. Always wanted a picture of the president? On a good day you can kiss it, on a bad day you can throw darts.

All you need to do is send a letter with your request to Presidential Correspondence, White House, Photo Department, Old Executive Office Building, Room 94, Washington, DC 20500; or online at http://www. whitehouse.gov

Bird-watching

It doesn't matter where you live. Just stand still and you will hear them; wild birds. Bird-watching is one of the fastest growing forms of outdoor recreation in the country. Each year millions of people discover for the first time the joys of bird-watching.

The U.S. Fish and Wildlife Service has published the booklet, *For The Birds*, where you can learn about the various types of bird food, nests, plants that attract birds, and more. For your copy or more information, contact Publications Unit, U.S. Fish and Wildlife Service, National Conservation Training Center, Rt. 1, Box 166, Shepherdstown, WV 25443; Carmina Olaya, 304-876-7203, Fax: 304-876-7689; or online at http://www.fws.gov

For your home

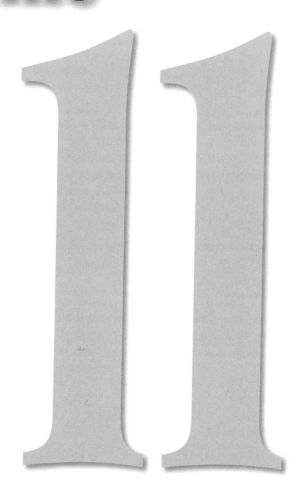

11

Chapter 11

For your home

Your newer old house

Looking for ways to restore, renovate, or just learn more about your old house? Every house contains clues to its original design and alterations, but how do you know what to look for?

The New Old House Starter Kit ($6) is one of the National Trust for Historic Preservation's information publications, a series of booklets on basic and frequently used preservation techniques.

Contact: Information, National Trust for Historic Preservation, 1785 Massachusetts Ave., NW, Washington, DC 20036; 202-588-6286; or online at http://www.nthp.org

Home shopping tips for veterans

Veterans can get an edge on the home buying market through use of a VA loan. The following three free publications can get you started on your house hunt.

Quick Guide to VA Home Loans is a guide for veterans whose home mortgage is guaranteed or insured under the GI Bill. *To the Home-buying Veteran* is a guide for veterans planning to buy or build homes with a VA loan.

VA-Guaranteed Home Loans for Veterans helps you understand what the VA can and cannot do for the home purchaser.

Contact: Veterans Assistance Office, U.S. Department of Veterans Affairs, 810 Vermont Ave., NW, Washington, DC 20420; 800-827-1000; or online at http://www.va.gov

Concerned about pesticides?

Do you use pesticides on your lawn or in your home? There are concerns about the dangers of pesticide use near people.

The U.S. Environmental Protection Agency (EPA) has several publications which provide the consumer with information concerning pesticides.

Some of the publications include:

- *Citizen's Guide to Pest Control and Pesticide Safety*—An informative brochure describing how to choose and use pesticides, how to pick a pest control company, and how to recognize a pesticide emergency and pesticide poisoning.

- *Healthy Lawn, Healthy Environment*—which explains how to care for your lawn in an environmentally friendly way.

- *EPA's Pesticide Programs*—pesticide registration and food safety are discussed first, followed by other pesticide programs.

Contact: National Center for Environmental Publications and Information, P.O. Box 42419, Cincinnati, OH 45242-2419; 800-490-9198; or online at http://www.epa.gov/ncepihom/

The masking tape deduction

You can write off many moving expenses if the conditions are politically correct and your motives are pure. You can even deduct expenses of moving back to the United States if you retire while living and working overseas.

Just call the Internal Revenue Service (IRS) and ask for *Publication 521, Moving Expenses*. You can contact them at 800-829-3676; or online at http://www.irs.gov/

Safe houses

To find a safe little hamlet to raise Junior, you better do some research before you move.

Uniform Crime Report, the Federal Bureau of Investigation's (FBI) annual report of violent and property crime, contains statistics for many towns with over 10,000 people, and can provide you with information such as the number of murders, robberies, assaults, burglaries, auto thefts, and more, but they do not rank cities.

Many libraries carry this publication, or you can call the FBI for information on your city.

Contact: Program Support Section, Federal Bureau of Investigation, Washington, DC 20535; or call 304-625-4995. You can also contact them online at http://www.fbi.gov/

Mortgage money guides

You have found your dream house, now what? You need to figure out how to pay for it. It is not as simple as it would seem. The Federal Trade Commission has several free publications dealing with the laws and regulations regarding getting a mortgage, mortgage servicing, mortgage refinancing, and what you need to look for when you are in the process.

The publications include: *Home Financing Primer, Using the Ads to Shop for Home Financing, Mortgage Servicing, Refinancing Your Home, Second Mortgage Financing*.

Contact: Public Reference, Room 130, Federal Trade Commission, Washington, DC 20580-0001; 202-326-2222; or online at http://www.ftc.gov

Free Christmas trees

For a small fee, the Bureau of Land Management issues permits to cut Christmas trees in the 11 Western states and Alaska. You will be given a map

with directions as to which areas are allowed for tree cutting.

Non-profit organizations can get trees for free, although this excludes the resale of trees. For more information check the blue pages of your phone book for your local Bureau of Land Management office or contact: Division of Forestry, Bureau of Land Management, U.S. Department of Interior, Washington, DC 20240, 202-452-7756; or online at http://www.blm.gov/

Before you even start looking for a house

Real estate brokers are everywhere. How do you know the good from the bad?

A free publication, *Real Estate Brokers*, provides a wealth of information regarding what the law requires for real estate brokers, your rights and responsibilities, as well as what to do when you have been unfairly treated.

Contact: Public Reference, Room 130, Federal Trade Commission, Washington, DC 20580-0001; 202-326-2222; or online at http://www.ftc.gov

This old house

Preservation of old homes is not an easy business. Finding weights and pulleys to repair old windows does not involve a simple trip to the hardware store. A free bibliography from the Government Printing Office titled *Buildings, Landmarks and Historic Sites of the United States* (SB-140) can get you started on your way to finding good resources for an authentic restoration.

Contact: Superintendent of Documents, Government Printing Office, Washington, DC 20402; 202-512-1800; or online at http://www.gpo.gov

Energy efficiency for you

The U.S. Department of Energy has a wide variety of information available regarding energy efficiency. It has information sheets on automatic and programmable thermostats, solar energy, appliance labeling, fans and ventilation, heat pumps, hot water conservation, insulation, as well as many more.

Two booklets that provide a wealth of information as well as some helpful suggestions include:

- *Tips For Saving Energy In Small Business*

- *Tips For An Energy Efficient Apartment*

All are free. Contact: Public Affairs, U.S. Department of Energy, Washington, DC 20585; 800-363-3732; or online at http://www.eren.doe.gov

Unseen, but deadly

Heard about the dangers of radon, but need to know more about it? *A Citizen's Guide to Radon* is a free booklet which helps readers understand the radon problem and decide if they need to take action to reduce radon levels in their homes. It explains what radon is, how it is detected, and what the results mean.

Contact: National Center for Environmental Publications and Information, P.O. Box 42419, Cincinnati, OH 45242-2419; 800-490-9198; or online at http://www.epa.gov/ncepihom/

Exactly what's it going to cost?

Buying a house can be an overwhelming experience. People are using a language you may never have heard before. Closing costs, mortgage lock-ins, settlement, title search, and more are all terms you need to know and fully understand before you sign on the dotted line.

The Federal Reserve has several free publications which will help you on your way to becoming an informed home buyer.

- *A Consumer's Guide to Mortgage Settlement Costs discusses closing costs, the title search, title insurance, and government-imposed costs.*

- *A Consumer's Guide to Mortgage Lock-Ins describes various aspects of mortgage lock-ins.*

- *A Consumer's Guide to Mortgage Refinancing explains the process and some of the risks and advantages to mortgage refinancing.*

Contact: Federal Reserve System, Board of Governors, Publications Services, MS-127, 20th St. and Constitution Ave., NW, Washington, DC 20551; 202-452-3244; or online at http://www.bog.frb.fed.us

Let me light your fire

Do you have a cabin in the woods with a woodstove, or are you thinking of installing one in your new home? Ask the U.S. Environmental Protection Agency (EPA) for some free advice.

Woodstoves can really help lower your heating bill, but you need to be sure that they are safe and effective. The Public Information Center has several free pamphlets on woodstoves including

- Fact Sheet: *Woodstoves; Up in Smoke*

- *Buying an EPA-Certified Woodstove*

- *Noncatalytic Woodstoves: Installation, Operation, and Maintenance*

- *Catalytic Woodstoves: Installation, Operation, and Maintenance.*

Contact: National Center for Environmental Publications and Information, P.O. Box 42419, Cincinnati, OH 45242-2419; 800-490-9198; or online at http://www.epa.gov/ncepihom/.

The EPA has a Wood Heater Program which can provide you with a current list of EPA-certified woodstoves as well as provide you with more information about wood burning and EPA's regulations.

They can be contacted at: Wood Heater Program (EN-341W), EPA, 401 M St., SW, Washington, DC 20460; 202-564-7091.

Pesticide safety

The pests have taken permanent residence in your home, so you reach for some chemical assistance in evicting the little creatures.

- *Pesticide Safety Tips* is a free fact sheet which gives helpful suggestions on pesticide use.

- *Pesticide Labels* discusses the parts of a label and what the information means.

- *Pesticides and Child Safety* lists recommendations for preventing accidental poisoning.

Contact: National Center for Environmental Publications and Information, P.O. Box 42419, Cincinnati, OH 45242-2419; 800-490-9198; or online at http://www.epa.gov/ncepihom/

For a different look

Suburbia may not be ready for this, but you could be. *Earth-Shelter Houses* is a free publication from the Energy Efficiency and Renewable Energy Clearinghouse, and provides information on different types of earth sheltered houses, their benefits, and information on where to go to learn more about this style of house.

Contact: Energy Efficiency and Renewable Energy Clearinghouse, P.O. Box 3048, Merrifield, VA 22116; 800-363-3732; or online at http://erecbbs.nciinc.com/

Make it as nature intended

Many do-it-yourselfers are looking at wood frame houses as a way to build their dream home. The Forest Service offers a free publication, *Wood Frame House Construction,* to get you sawing.

Contact: Forest Service, U.S. Department of Agriculture, Attention: Public Affairs Office, P.O. Box 9060, Washington, DC 20090-6090; 202-205-0957; or online at http://www.fs.fed.us/

Counseling for homebuyers, homeowners, and tenants

To help reduce delinquencies, defaults, and foreclosures, the U.S. Department of Housing and Urban Development (HUD) provides free counseling to homeowners and tenants under its programs through HUD-approved counseling agencies.

The counselors advise and assist homeowners with budgeting, money management, and buying and maintaining their homes. This is not just for HUD homes, but for all home buyers and owners. The amount of service available does vary for each counseling agency.

Contact your local HUD office for the counseling agency nearest you.

Contact: Single Family Servicing Division, Secretary-Held and Counseling Services, Office of Insured Single Family Housing, U.S. Department of Housing and Urban Development (HUD), Washington, DC 20410-8000; 800-569-4287; or online at http://www.hudhcc.org

Pest-free home

Tired of calling the bug man? Worried about the chemicals used to rid your home of pests? The U.S. Environmental Protection Agency has several free environmental fact sheets on pesticide and pesticide safety.

- *Preventing Pests In Your Home* provides tips on general prevention methods and resources for more information.

- National Pesticide Telecommunications Network (NPTN) provides a wide variety of pesticide-related information as well as a toll-free number for further information.

Contact: National Center for Environmental Publications and Information, P.O. Box 42419, Cincinnati, OH 45242-2419; 800-490-9198; or online at http://www.epa.gov/ncepihom/

Efficient houses

Houses are expensive enough. Learn how you can improve the efficiency of your home from the Energy Efficiency and Renewable Energy Clearinghouse, which covers such topics as active/passive solar, solar thermal, photovoltaics, wind, biomass, alcohol fuels, hydroelectric, geothermal, and ocean thermal energy.

Some of the free publications include:

- *Guide to Making Energy-Smart Purchases*

- *Solar Water Heating*

- *Cooling Your Home Naturally*

- *Skylights for Residences*

- *Home Energy Audits*

- *Solar and Energy-Efficient House Plans*

- *Radiant Floor Heating*

- *Estimating Payback for Additional Insulation*

For these publications and information on others available contact: Energy Efficiency and Renewable Energy Clearinghouse, P.O. Box 3048, Merrifield, VA 22116; 800-363-3732; or online at http://erecbbs.nciinc.com/

For your investments

For your
investments

Chapter

For your investments

Your own investment counselor

The Securities and Exchange Commission are the guys who write the rules and regulations and provide protection for investors, making sure that the securities markets are safe and honest.

They have a free publication, *Invest Wisely,* which contains basic information on choosing investments and keeping them safe, trading securities, and different protections guaranteed by law.

Contact: Publications Section, U.S. Securities and Exchange Commission, 450 5th St., NW, Washington, DC 20549; 202-942-4040; or online at http://www.sec.gov

Credit handbook

Worried about your credit rating? Need some advice about restoring your credit? *The Consumer Handbook To Credit Protection Laws*, can help you understand how the credit protection laws can help you, and is available free from this office.

Contact: Publications Services, MS-127, Federal Reserve Board, Washington, DC 20551; 202-452-3244; or online at http://www.bog. frb.fed.us

Save with savings bonds

Trying to save for your kids' education? *Investor's Guide* (SBD 2085) describes the information you need to purchase savings bonds, such as available series and denominations, interest rates, where to buy, registration, annual limitation on purchases, redemption, tax status, exchange of series HH bonds, and safety features.

Contact: Office of Public Affairs, U.S. Savings Bonds Marketing Office, U.S. Department of the Treasury, 999 E St., Washington, DC 20226; 202-219-4235; or online at http://www.savingsbonds.gov

Save for the future with futures

Thinking of moving into the futures market? What things do you need to know before you invest? The Commodity Futures Trading Commission (CFTC) can provide studies of the function of futures markets. They also have free

reports and publications about the Commission, as well as information on commodities futures trading. Some of the free information includes: *CFTC Annual Report,* and *Economic Purposes of Futures Trading*.

Contact: Office of Public Affairs, Commodity Futures Trading Commission (CFTC), 3 Lafayette Centre, 1155 21st St., NW, Washington, DC 20581; 202-418-5080; or online at http://www.cftc.gov

Commemorative coins bring big bucks

Commemorative coins have become a way to raise money for a particular national cause. The 1986 Statue of Liberty coins raised $83 million. These are just a few of the facts available in *A Brief History of the United States Mint.*

For your free copy contact: United States Mint, 633 Third St., NW, Washington, DC 20220; 202-874-6450; or online at http://www.ustreas.gov/ treasury/bureaus/ mint/mint.html

Van Gogh for $1,000?

A friend of a friend knows where you can get an original Van Gogh for $1,000, and he swears he found it in his grandmother's attic. How can you be sure it's for real? The FBI will run a check of the National Stolen Art File, a computer list of all the currently missing works of art reported as stolen in the U.S., and let you know if the painting is hot or not.

Contact: National Stolen Art File, Federal Bureau of Investigation, U.S. Department of Justice, Washington, DC 20535; 202-324-4192.

Minerals into money

The U.S. Geological Survey conducts research in the areas of mining, processing, and materials technology, with an emphasis on health and safety, mining efficiency, environmental concerns, and energy and materials conservation. There is information available on all the different minerals, as well as a publication called *Mineral Commodity Summaries* ($17) which comes out annually and has interesting facts about different commodities.

Call or write for any of the free publications: Superintendent of Documents, U.S. Government Printing Office, P.O. Box 371954, Pittsburgh, PA 15250-1954; 202-512-1800; or online at http://www.gpo.gov

Get rich quick schemes

How quick can you get rich investing in a pyramid scheme? How quickly can you lose your shirt? The Securities and Exchange Commission can send you the following free publications to help you protect your investments:

• *Ask Questions*

• *What Every Investor Should Know*

• *Investment Fraud and Abuse Travel to Cyberspace*

Contact: Publications Section, U.S. Securities and Exchange Commission, Washington, DC 20549; 202-942-4040; or online at http://www.sec.gov

Did your broker make you broke?

Are you having some problems with your brokerage firm regarding fees or money? *Arbitration Procedures* is a free publication which discusses procedures for disputes with brokerage firms involving financial claims.

Contact: Publications Section, U.S. Securities and Exchange Commission, Washington, DC 20549; 202-942-4040; or online at http://www.sec.gov

For your kids

13

Chapter 13

For your kids

Shake it up baby!

Are earthquakes your thing? Contact the U.S. Geological Survey for free publications, such as, *Earthquakes, The Severity of an Earthquake,* and *The San Andreas Fault,* all of which are free and provide a wealth of information on a very shaky subject.

You can learn how earthquakes start, what to do when one occurs, and what area of the country is most likely to experience tremors.

Contact: U.S. Geological Survey, P.O. Box 25286, Denver, CO 80225; 800-USA-MAPS; or online at http://www.usgs.gov/

Do you like to second guess the Weather Channel?

The National Oceanic and Atmospheric Administration can provide you with information on keeping a weather log, weather warnings and more. *Watch Out...Storms Ahead! Owlie Skywarn's Weather Book* is a fun book describing different weather conditions.

Contact your local weather service office to get a single copy, or contact: Educational Programs Branch, National Oceanic and Atmospheric

Administration, 1825 Connecticut Ave., NW, Washington, DC 20235; 301-713-0090, ext. 118; or online at http://www.nws.noaa.gov

Step out of the way

Volcanoes can erupt at any time. Remember Mount St. Helens? The U.S.

Geological Survey has two free publications that explain how volcanoes are formed, why they erupt and more.

Request *Volcanic Hazards at Mount Shasta, California,* and *Volcanoes of the United States* by writing U.S. Geological Survey, P.O. Box 25286, Denver, CO 80225; 800-USA-MAPS; or online at http://www.usgs.gov/

Money, money, money

Did you know that 95% of the notes printed each year are used to replace notes already in circulation; that 48% of the notes printed are $1 notes?

You can learn a lot about your money from the Bureau of Engraving and Printing. Some information sheets available include:

- *The Money Factory,* which describes how money is made.

- *Mutilated Currency,* which describes what happens to old, worn out bills.

- *Fun Facts about Dollars,* on money trivia.

- *The Story of Money.*

Contact: Bureau of Engraving and Printing, U.S. Department of the Treasury, 14th and C Sts., SW, Washington, DC 20228; 202-874-3019; or online at http://www.bep.treas.gov/

Water

We all drink it, but what exactly is it? The U.S. Geological Survey can provide you with many free publications that explain water, water usage, and water contamination. Some of the titles include:

- *Water: The Resource That Gets Used and Used and Used for Everything!*

- *How Do We Treat Our Wastewater?*

- *Watersheds: Where We Live.*

- *Groundwater: The Hidden Resource!*

Contact: U.S. Geological Survey, P.O. Box 25286, Denver, CO 80225; 800-USA-MAPS; or online at http://www.usgs.gov/education/

Give a hoot! Don't pollute!

The Woodsy Owl Activity Guide is filled with dozens of ideas for classroom activities, a list of kid's books, tags, badges and more.

Contact: The Smokey Bear-Woodsy Owl Center of Excellence, 402 SE 11th St., Grand Rapids, MN 55744; or online at http://www.fs.fed.us/woodsy/

Let the sun shine in

People are trying to find new ways to heat their homes, factories, offices and schools without using expensive oil and gas. *Solar Energy and You* helps teach you about solar energy and solar heat. They also have other publications for kids dealing with alternative energy sources.

Contact: Energy Efficiency and Renewable Energy Clearinghouse, P.O. Box 3048, Merrifield, VA 22116; 800-363-3732; or online at http://erecbbs.nciinc.com/

Help your kids hit the books

Every child learns in his or her own way. To help encourage children to excel in school, the U.S. Department of Education has developed the *Help Your Child* series, to teach parents strategies they can use every day to teach their children to read, learn geography, even to use the library.

The free series include:

- *Helping Your Child Learn to Read*

- *Helping Your Child Succeed in School*

- *Help Your Child Learn to Write Well*

- *Help Your Child Learn Geography*

- *Helping Your Child Learn Science*

- *Helping Your Child Use the Library*

- *Helping Your Child Get Ready for School*

- *Helping Your Child Learn Math*

Contact: U.S. Department of Education, Office of Educational Research and Improvement, 555 New Jersey Ave., NW, Washington, DC 20208-5721; 800-424-1616; or online at http://www.ed.gov/pubs/parents.html

Send your kids to the moon

Looking for an interesting way for your kids to spend summer vacation? Space Camp is a way for them to learn about science, planets, rocketry, and more at the Space and Rocket Center. It does cost to send your kids to camp, but a scholarship program is available where kids can go for free.

To apply for this program kids need to complete an application, write a one-page essay, and have a teacher recommendation.

For an information packet on Space Camp and a scholarship application contact: Space and Rocket Center, One Tranquillity Base, Huntsville, AL 35807; 800-63-SPACE; or online at http://www.spacecamp.com/

Read me a story

Reading Is Fundamental is a program designed to encourage children of all ages to read and to help distribute books to those who can't afford them. They have developed a series of brochures ($1 each) which deal with a variety of reading topics. Some of these include:

- *Building a Family Library*

- *Choosing Good Books For Your Children*

- *Encouraging Soon-to-Be Readers*

- *Reading Aloud to Your Children*

- *Summertime Reading*

- *Upbeat and Offbeat Activities to Encourage Reading.*

To order these and to find out about other information available contact the Reading Is Fundamental program.

Contact: Reading Is Fundamental, Publications Department, 600 Maryland Ave., SW, Suite 600, Washington, DC 20024; 202-287-3371; or online at http://www.si.edu/rif

For your little scout

The president always likes a good cause. Girl Scouts and Boy Scouts are worthy of notice, so let the White House know of your special scout and president Bill will send a certificate.

Contact: White House, Greetings Office, 1600 Pennsylvania Ave., NW, Washington, DC 20500.

How old is the tree out front?

Tree Rings: Timekeepers of the Past explains how past environmental conditions have been recorded in tree rings and how scientists interpret this information.

Contact: U.S. Geological Survey, P.O. Box 25286, Denver, CO 80225; 800-USA-MAPS; or online at http://www.usgs.gov/

Get in shape a fun way

The kids need to get off the couch and get outside. *Get Fit! A Handbook for Youth Ages 6-17* will help them become as physically fit as they can be.

For more information, contact The President's Council on Physical Fitness and Sports, 200 Independence Ave., SW, Humphrey Bldg., Room 738H, Washington, DC 20201; 202-690-9000, Fax: 202-690-5211; or online at http://www.indiana.edu/~preschal/

The school bus is not a zoo

Get thirty kids together in a confined space, and a circus can occur at the drop of a hat.

Teach your kids important bus safety rules through a free fact sheet titled *Kids, The School Bus, and You*. Your kids spend a lot of time on the bus, so make sure they arrive at school and home safely by reviewing the rules. Your bus driver will thank you.

Contact: National Highway Traffic Safety Administration, Auto Safety Hotline NEF-11.2HL, 400 Seventh St., SW, Washington, DC 20590; 800-424-9393; or online at http://www.nhtsa.dot.gov

Safety first

Kids love to go to the park, but often forget safety rules while there. *Little Big Kids* (for ages 3-5) assists children in learning safe play habits on the playground and reinforces those lessons.

Write: U.S. Consumer Product Safety Commission (CPSC), Publication Request, Washington, DC 20207; 800-638-CPSC; or online at http://www.cpsc.gov/

Shopping made safe

Toys are supposed to be fun, not dangerous. The U.S. Consumer Product Safety Commission's mission is to protect the public from unreasonable risks of injury and death associated with consumer products.

They have published a series of publications dealing with toy safety including:

- *Toy Boxes and Toy Chests Fact Sheet* (#074)

- *Baby Product Safety Alert* (#250)

- *For Kids Sake, Think Toy Safety Pamphlet* (#4281)

- *Toy Safety Coloring Book* (#283)

For your free copies or a complete publications list, write: U.S. Consumer Product Safety Commission (CPSC), Publication Request, Washington, DC 20207; 800-638-CPSC; or online at http://www.cpsc.gov

Help them to read

In order to help their children succeed, parents need to encourage and help their kids become good readers. The ERIC Clearinghouse on Reading and Communication Skills provides information in the fields of reading, writing, English, literacy, and more. They publish a series of parent booklets to encourage family involvement, which include:

- *How Can I Improve My Child's Reading?*

- *101 Ideas to Help Your Child Learn to Read and Write*

• *Teaching Critical Reading through Literature* (D86)

• *Reading and Writing in a Kindergarten Classroom* (D63)

• *Beginning Reading Instruction in the United States* (D57)

• *How Well Do Tests Measure Real Reading?* (D41)

For a complete list of publications and more information, contact: ERIC Clearinghouse on Reading and Communication Skills, Indiana University, Smith Research Center, P.O. Box 5953, Bloomington, IN 47407; 812-855-5847; or online at http://www.indiana.edu/~eric_rec/

Ready for kindergarten?

Raising kids is no easy job, but there is some help available through the ERIC Clearinghouse for Elementary and Early Childhood Education.

This Clearinghouse encompasses the physical, social, and educational development of children from birth through early adolescence. They publish a free newsletter which describes the latest research in the field and other related information.

The Clearinghouse also makes available ERIC Digests which are concise reports on timely issues. These are free, but please include a self-addressed stamped envelope. Some of the titles include:

• *Readiness: Children and Schools*

• *Infant Child Care*

• *Approaches to School-Age Child Care*

• *Measuring Kindergartners' Social Competence*

• *Positive Discipline*

For these and other information contact: ERIC Clearinghouse for Elementary and Early Childhood Education, University of Illinois, College of Education, 805 West Pennsylvania Ave., Urbana, IL 61801; 800-583-4135; or online at http://ericps.crc.vivc.edu/ericeece.html

A view from above

Show your kids the real thing when they ask about space. Free pictures with a synopsis on the back are great teaching tools for children or that obsessive space person. Stickers are also available for various space shuttles.

Some of the pictures include your favorite space shuttle mission and:

• *The First "Solo" in Space*

• *The Endeavor*

• *Apollo 17's View of Earth*

Don't miss out. To get your pictures, call or write to the NASA Teacher Resource Center (TRC) nearest you. To find the closest TRC, call NASA Publications Center, 202-554-4380; or online at http://www.nasa.gov

Helmets are the rule

It is such a thrill to learn how to ride a bike without training wheels, but bikes are involved in over 500,000 injuries.

Teach your kids to ride safely through two free publications available from the U.S. Consumer Product Safety Commission. *Sprocketman Comic Book* (#341) and *Ten Smart Routes to Bike Safety* (#343) can both help your kids have a great and safe time bicycling.

For your free copies write: Consumer Product Safety Commission (CPSC), Publication Request, Washington, DC 20207; 800-638-CPSC; or online at http://www.cpsc.gov/

Inside volcanoes

If your kids like things that explode (and who doesn't), get "Inside Volcanoes", an award-winning poster juxtaposing images of Mount St. Helens and Kilauea with artistic manipulation to convey the excitement of volcanic activity. The 36" by 23" poster is available for $5 (plus $4 s/h).

Contact: Smithsonian Institution Traveling Exhibition Service, Publications Department, Department 0564, Washington, DC 20073; 202-357-1338; or online at http://www.si.edu/organiza/offices/sites/start.htm

A prehistoric magazine

Dinosaurs may be extinct, but that makes them all the more fascinating to kids. Now there's a magazine devoted to these lovely creatures.

Zinj helps capture the fascination kids have for dinosaurs and other "old stuff" by showing them that paleontology, archeology, and anthropology are fun and exciting. The full-color, hero sized, quarterly magazine, is supported by a consortium of federal and state agencies, and is written with kid input. Subscriptions are available for $12 per year (make check payable to Zinj).

Contact: Zinj Magazine, 358 South Rio Grande, Salt Lake City, UT 84101, 801-533-8808, Fax: 801-533-3503.

Color me

Teach your kids about the world around them with two great coloring books. *My Wetland Coloring Book* ($3.25) introduces children to drawings of swamps, marshes, bogs, and other kinds of wetlands. *Endangered Species Coloring Book: Save Our Species* ($2.25) contains more than 23 drawings illustrating endangered species in their natural habitat.

For your copies contact: Superintendent of Documents, U.S. Government Printing Office, P.O. Box 371954, Pittsburgh, PA 15250-7954; 202-512-1800; or online at http://www.gpo.gov/

Listen to your elders

Words of wisdom make more of an impression when you get them directly from the source.

The Grand Generation: Interviewing Guide and Questionnaire ($1.50) lists guidelines for collecting folklore and oral history from older tradition-bearers. It includes a general guide to conducting interviews, a list of sample questions, and examples of ways to preserve and present findings.

Family Folklore Interviewing Guide and Questionnaire ($1.75) is a guide to collecting family folklore, including background information on the importance of recording it, details on techniques and presentation, and a sample questionnaire.

Contact: Smithsonian Institution Traveling Exhibition Service (SITES), Publications Department, Department 0564, Washington, DC 20073; 202-357-1338 (include $4 shipping and handling); or online at http://www.si.edu/organiza/offices/sites/start.htm

Get out the crayons

Teach your kids about the environment in a fun way. The U.S. Environmental Protection Agency has a number of coloring books to help you increase your child's awareness of the Earth.

- *The Happy Earth Day Coloring and Activities Book*

- *Superfund for Kids Coloring Book*

- *Adventures of the Garbage Gremlin: Recycle and Combat a Life of Grime*

- *Sammy Soil: A Coloring Book Story*

- *My Radon Coloring Book*

- *A World Fit for Chipmunks and Other Living Things*

For your free copies contact: U.S. Environmental Protection Agency, Information Access Branch, Public Information Center, 401 M St., SW, 3404, Washington, DC 20460; 800-490-9198; or online at http://www.epa.gov/kids/

Solar system puzzle

Want to help your child build a solar system? "Solar System Puzzle Kit" is an activity book for parents and children which includes patterns and supplemental materials. Kids are asked to assemble an eight-cube paper puzzle, and when solved, they can create a miniature solar system.

Call or write your request to the NASA Teacher Resource Center nearest you. To find the closest TRC, call NASA Publications Center at 202-554-4380; or online at http://windows.ivv.nasa.gov/teacher_resources/activity.html

Images from space

National Aeronautics and Space Administration (NASA) offers many incredible posters of images from space and more, free of charge.

To get your posters, call or write to the NASA Teacher Resource Center (TRC) nearest you. To find the closest TRC, call NASA Publications Center, 202-554-4380; or online at http://www.nasa.gov/

For your love life

Chapter 14
For your love life

The marriage-go-round

Check out the singles scene anywhere in the country by contacting the Bureau of the Census, which keeps some interesting figures regarding the population, such as the ratio of total number of single men to single women in metro areas.

Give them a call to find out what areas of the country will improve your chances of finding that special someone.

Contact: Marriage and Family Statistics, Population Division, Bureau of the Census, Bldg. 3, Room 2353, Washington, DC 20233; 301-457-2465, 301-457-2416; or online at http://www.census.gov/

Is marrying a millionaire a dream come true?

The first step is finding one.

The Internal Revenue Service has some interesting statistics, including the top three states with millionaire residents (California, New York, and Florida).

For more information contact: Acting Director of Statistics, Statistics Income Division, EP:S, Internal Revenue Service, P.O. Box 2608, Washington, DC 20013, 202-874-0410; or online at http://www.irs.gov/

Impotence...when love's a letdown

Many types of sexual dysfunction can now be treated.

Some 10 million men suffer from impotence, so the National Kidney and Urologic Diseases Information Clearinghouse has developed a free "Impotence Information Fact Sheet," which includes articles and literature searches on the causes and cures for impotence and examines the pros and cons of different types of penile implants.

Contact: National Kidney and Urologic Diseases Information Clearinghouse, 3 Information Way, Bethesda, MD 20892-3580; 301-654-4415; or online at http://www.niddk.nih.gov/brochures/nkudic.htm

The top nine

The Food and Drug Administration (FDA) regulates drugs and medical devices to ensure that they are safe and effective. They publish *Consumer-Friendly Birth Control Information*, which discusses the possible side effects and effectiveness of 17 different types of birth control.

Another free publication is *Protecting Against Unintended Pregnancy: A Guide to Contraceptive Choices,* a more detailed look at the options and risks.

Contact: Office of Consumer Affairs, Food and Drug Administration, 5600 Fishers Lane, HFE-88, Rockville, MD 20857; 800-532-4440; or online at http://www.fda.gov/

The condom people

The Food and Drug Administration regulates condoms to make sure they are both safe and effective.

The Consumer Affairs Office can provide you with information on the effectiveness of condoms in the prevention of the spread of AIDS and more. Some of their free publications include:

- *Condoms and Sexually Transmitted Diseases... Especially AIDS*

- *Letter to: All U.S. Condom Manufacturers, Importers and Repackagers of Condoms*

Contact: Division of Consumer Affairs, Center for Devices and Radiological Health, 5600 Fishers Lane, HFZ-210, Rockville, MD 20857; 301-443-4190; or online at http://www.fda.gov/

Bigger breasts: Sure, but how safe?

Seems like each week the newspaper runs some story regarding the dangers of silicone gel-filled breast implants.

To get the facts on these implants and under what conditions implants are still permitted contact the Food and Drug Administration's Breast Implant Hotline.

You can request a free "Breast Implants Information" packet, which includes information on clinical trials and regulations concerning breast implants.

Contact: Center for Devices and Radiological Health, Food and Drug Administration, 5600 Fishers Lane, Rockville, MD 20857; 800-532-4440; or online at http://www.fda.gov/

AIDS: Changing sex practices

Are you concerned about AIDS? What risks are you taking in having sex? There is so much information out there regarding AIDS, how do you know what is true?

The AIDS Clearinghouse can answer all your questions, refer you to testing centers, link you with support groups, send you publications, reports, posters, and more. Some of the free publications include:

• *Voluntary HIV Counseling and Testing: Facts, Issues, and Answers*

• *Surgeon General's Report to the American Public on HIV Infection and AIDS*

• *HIV Infection and AIDS: Are You at Risk?*

Contact: National AIDS Information Clearinghouse, P.O. Box 6003, Rockville, MD 20849; 800-458-5231; or online at http://www.cdcnac.org/

Are your hot flashes getting hotter?

Menopause doesn't have to be the hormonal hurricane women faced in the past.

Taking estrogen and progesterone can help relieve the problems of menopause, although they are not without problems of their own.

A free booklet entitled, *Menopause*, can answer many of your questions and outlines different forms of treatment.

Contact: National Institute on Aging, P.O. Box 8057, Gaithersburg, MD 20898; 800-222-2225; or online at http://www.nih.gov/nia/

Free condoms!

Now there is no excuse. Title X Family Planning Clinics will provide free condoms and other birth control devices to people who meet certain income level requirements.

These clinics will also provide physical examinations (including testing for cancer and sexually transmitted diseases), infertility services, services for adolescents, pregnancy tests, periodic follow-up examinations, referral to and from other social and medical services agencies, and ancillary services.

To locate a clinic near you or to request a publication, contact: Office of Population Affairs Clearinghouse P.O. Box 30686, Bethesda, MD 20824-0686; 301-654-6190; or online at http://www.hhs.gov/progorg/opa/clearing.html

Norplant—the latest thing

This Center can provide you with free reports and information regarding the new contraceptive called Norplant. Reports include information on patient labeling, prescribing, usage, warnings, and Food and Drug Administration (FDA) statements regarding Norplant. There is a free FDA consumer article detailing the pros and cons of Norplant.

Contact: Center for Drug Evaluation and Research, HFD-8, Food and Drug Administration, 5600 Fishers Lane, Rockville, MD 20857; 800-532-4440; or online at http://www.fda.gov/

Contraceptive risk and effectiveness—get the facts

The National Institute of Child Health and Human Development distributes pamphlets and reports on various methods of contraception, as well as medical updates on the risks and/or effectiveness of new forms of birth control.

Two of their free publications include:

- *Facts About Oral Contraceptives* which describes different forms of contraception

- *Facts About Vasectomy Safety* which describes vasectomies. Contact the Institute for more information on contraception.

Contact: National Institute of Child Health and Human Development, National Institutes of Health (NIH), Building 31, Room 2A32, 9000 Rockville Pike, Bethesda, MD 20892; 301-496-5133; or online at http://www.nih.gov/nichd/

Fearless sex hotline

Sexually transmitted diseases (STD) are nothing new. From Casanova to Sigmund Freud, some of the greatest lovers of all times had to pay for not being careful.

The Sexually Transmitted Diseases hotline can give you the latest information on a wide range of STDs and how to protect yourself. Some of the free publications include:

- *Condoms, Contraceptives and Sexually Transmitted Disease*—discusses how some forms of birth control protect against STDs.

- *Protect Yourself and Your Baby From Sexually Transmitted Disease* —explains the dangers of STDs for unborn babies.

- *STDs: What You Should Know*—answers some basic questions on STDs.

Contact: National Sexually Transmitted Diseases Hotline, P.O. Box 13827, Research Triangle Park, NC 27709; 800-227-8922; or online at http://sunsite. unc.edu/asha/

Holland is for lovers

Are you thinking of making your nuptials one for the memory books? Maybe an overseas wedding would make your special day unforgettable.

The Department of State has an information sheet titled, *Marriage of U.S. Citizens Abroad*, which explains what you need to do to make it legal. Contact: Office of Citizens Counselor, U.S. Department of State, Room 4811, 2201 C St., NW, Washington, DC 20520, 202-647-4000; or online at http://206.161.1096/marriage.html

Honeymoon planning made simple

Don't know where to go or how to get there? No problem.

Every state operates a travel and tourism office, and almost all have toll-free numbers. These hotlines can provide you with a wealth of information, including where to stay, what to do, where to eat, current events and festivals, maps, and more. All this can be delivered to your door for free.

Contact Information for the phone listing in your capital, or you can view a list of travel offices by looking at http://www.pueblo.gsa.gov/cic_text/trav&hob/travel.txt

For your mantel

Chapter 15

For your mantel

Superheros, for real

The Congressional Medal of Honor is awarded to those members of the Armed Services whose actions against the enemy go above and beyond the call of duty. Past winners include Buffalo Bill Cody and Dr. Mary Walker, who was a Civil War surgeon and the first and only female to receive the award.

For information concerning this and other medals and decoration of the Armed Forces contact: Public Affairs, U.S. Department of Defense, Room 2E777, The Pentagon, Washington, DC 20301-1400; 703-697-5737.

And the Emmy for exports goes to...

Superpowers these days fight over commodities and trade barriers, armed with fax, phone, and the latest figures. The President's "E" Award and the "E Star" Award for Excellence in Exporting is designed to honor American exporters, who demonstrate breakthroughs in competitive markets and the overcoming of export problems. Some past winners include Karsten Manufacturing Corp. for Ping Golf Clubs, Coleman Company, and Frymaster Corporation.

For more information contact: "E" Award Program Officer, Office of Domestic Operation, U.S. and Foreign Commercial Service, ITA, U.S. Department of Commerce, Room 3810, Washington, DC 20230; 202-482-1289; or online at http://www.ita.doc.gov/

When the little guy sees big

While corporate giants are downsizing to beat the band, scores of dynamic small businesses are busy building America's tomorrow. If you know of an innovative small business owner in your state, then nominate him/her for The Small Business Person of the Year award. Other categories include minority, women, or veterans small business, exporter, young entrepreneur, and even for federal government contractor or subcontractor of the year.

For more information on these awards contact: Your local SBA office, or the Answer Desk, U.S. Small Business Administration, 409 3rd. St., SW, Washington, DC 20416; 800-8-ASK-SBA; or online at http://www.sba.gov/

Recognize the best

Unlike the universe, science and math didn't just happen. The Presidential Awards For Excellence In Science And Mathematics Teaching recognizes this, and is open to teachers in grades kindergarten through 12th grade. This award includes a $7,500 grant to the awardee's school and a free trip to Washington.

For more information contact: Presidential Awards For Excellence In Science And Mathematics Teaching, National Science Teachers Association, 1840 Wilson Blvd., Arlington, VA 22201-3000; 703-243-7100. Fax: 703-243-7177; or online at http://www.nsta.org/

Bringing technology to the common man

Which came first, the popsicle or the stick? Inventors may come up with great ideas, but getting them to market takes technical know-how. National Medal of Technology is given to a U.S. citizen or company which excels in the commercialization of technology. Past winners include Del Meyer, the man who brought us polyester, and Bill Gates from Microsoft.

For an application contact: U.S. Department of Commerce, Technology Administration, Dr. Paul Braden, National Medal of Technology, Room 4418, 14th St. and Constitution Ave., NW, Washington, DC 20230; 202-482-5572; or online at http://www.ta.doc.gov/medal/

Be true to your school

The Blue Ribbon School Award is given by the U.S. Department of Education to award schools that excel in educational leadership, instruction, organization, and parental and community involvement. Schools are asked to report their progress toward achieving the National Education Goals and to describe in detail the school program.

For more information contact: U.S. Department of Education, Knowledge Applications Division, Blue Ribbon Schools Program, Washington, DC 20208-5645; 202-219-2149; or online at http://www.ed.gov/

Beam me up, Scotty

Space holds a special fascination for kids and there are several special award programs to keep that interest on the front burner.

Both NASA and the National Science Teachers Association sponsor competitions for would-be skywalkers.

- The Interplanetary Art Competition (grades 3-12) is for students who have a vision of interplanetary space, including a description.

- Future Aircraft/Spacecraft Design (grades 3-5) encourages students working in teams to design aircraft.

For guidelines, information, and application procedures contact: National Science Teachers Association, 1840 Wilson Boulevard, Arlington, VA 22201; 703-243-7100, Fax: 703-243-7177; or online at http://www.nsta.org/

It's just gas

Come up with a novel way to expand U.S. fossil fuel reserves without stepping on Mrs. Nature's toes and everyone wins but the Iraqis.

The Lowry Award winners work to find ways to expand the U.S.'s finite gas, coal and oil reserves in an environmentally responsible manner with winners receiving a gold medal, citation, and $10,000.

For nominations procedures contact: Awards Officer, FE-72, Office of Fossil Energy, Attn: Fred Glaser, U.S. Department of Energy, Washington, DC 20585; 301-903-2786; or online at http://www.fe.doe.gov/

Start by jogging your dog

Not everyone has time to become an Olympic-class athlete, but that doesn't mean you can't compete. Take the President's Challenge, which is a physical fitness testing program of the President's Council on Physical Fitness and Sports with schools nationwide participating in the program. Anyone age

6 to 96 can also earn the Presidential Sports Award in any one of 68 activities, and there is even a Family Fitness Award.

To learn how to be a winner contact: The President's Council on Physical Fitness and Sports, 701 Pennsylvania Ave., NW, Suite 250, Washington, DC 20004; 202-272-3430 or 202-272-3431; or online at http://www.indiana.edu/~preschal/index.html

Uncle Sam's star awards

Space Science Student Involvement Program (SSIP) is an annual program that involves students in creating experiments, art, and writing in areas of interest to NASA.

- Mission To Planet Earth (grades 6-8) allows teams to develop a project that uses satellites to determine effect of human activity on Earth.

- Mars Science Experiment Project (grades 9-12) asks students to design an expedition to Mars.

- Aerospace Internship Competition (grades 9-12) requires students to design experiments that could be theoretically performed in a NASA center.

For guidelines, information, and application procedures contact: National Science Teachers Association, 1840 Wilson Blvd., Arlington, VA 22201; 703-243-7100, Fax: 703-243-7177; or online at http://www.nsta.org/programs/sst/ssip/ssipbrch.shtml

Honors for a class act

Getting kids to think creatively and critically is something we all want to encourage.

The Quigg Excellence in Education Award is presented to teachers, students, parents, or others that encourage this kind of analytical thinking in America's youth. You can win for a single specific event or for a series of activities which get America's youth inventing.

Contact: Project XL, Office of Public Affairs, The Patent and Trademark Office, Washington, DC 20231; 703-305-8341; or online at http://www.uspto.gov/

Grade the principal

To reward people who have devoted their careers to other people's children, the U.S. Department of Education and the National Association of Elementary School Principals (NAESP) present awards to National Distinguished Principals. The guidelines include nomination and selection by peers, demonstrated commitment to excellence, evidence of support, high standards and expectations for students and staff, and service as a principal for at least five years.

For more information contact: National Association of Elementary School Principals, 1615 Duke St., Alexandria, VA 22314; 703-684-3345, 800-38-NAESP; or online at http://www.naesp.org/

Intellectual athletics

Some students would rather compete on the blackboard than on the gridiron, but that doesn't make them geeks. It makes them tomorrow's Oxford scholars and possible presidential material. The White House and the U.S. Department of Education recognize these students through the Presidential Scholars awards program for both academic and art scholars.

For more information contact: The White House, Commission on Presidential Scholars, U.S. Department of Education, 400 Maryland Avenue, SW,

Room 5101, Washington, DC 20202; 202-401-1365; or online at http://www.whitehouse.gov/.

Top ten quality control freaks

Think your company is tops when it comes to quality? For quality awareness and strategies, the Malcolm Baldrige National Quality Award may be given annually in each of three categories: manufacturing, service, and small business. Applicants must undergo a rigorous evaluation by an independent board and be judged in many different areas. In fact, many executives use the Baldrige criteria to establish quality improvement programs in their companies. Past winners include AT&T Network Systems Group, The Ritz-Carlton Hotel Co., and Federal Express Corp.

For more information contact: Malcolm Baldrige National Quality Award Office, A537 Administration Building, National Institute of Standards and Technology, Gaithersburg, MD 20899-0001; 301-975-2036; Fax: 301-948-3716; or online at:

http://www.quality.nist.gov

For your mind

Chapter 16

For your mind

News of the day

Is this a good time to open your dream restaurant, Cafe, Tea, and Me? What about building your country house?

This U.S. Department of Commerce recorded message provides you with the latest numbers on monthly housing completions, composite indexes, leading economic indicators, wholesale and retail sales and more.

Call: Commerce Department News: 202-606-5306 for gross domestic products; 202-606-5303 for personal income; 202-606-5362 for international transactions; or online at http://www.doc.gov/

All aboard

Kids love to watch planes, trains, and ships. You can call this recorded message to find which ships and barges are coming and going, as well as their departure times.

Call: St. Lawrence Seaway Ship Arrival Message Line; 905-688-6462; or online at http://www.seaway.ca/

Better than a Rolex

Tired of being late? Did your grandmother teach you that punctuality is a virtue? Set your watch to the exact time of the Atomic Clock at the Naval Observatory, and see how you do.

Call: Time (within milliseconds); 202-762-1401; or online at http://tycho.usno.navy.mil/cgi_bin/timer.pl

How much can you really take with you?

This Pension Benefit Guaranty Corporation message provides you with interest rates for valuing benefits and pension plans, so you can plan your retirement in style.

Call: Pension Plans and Interest Rates Message Line; 202-326-4041; or online at http://www.pbgc.gov/

How much?

Let Uncle Sam set your prices for you. The government tracks the prices of specific products each month and then releases the price changes in the form of the producer price index. All you need to do is follow the trend of the U.S. Department of Labor.

Call: Producer Price Index Message Line; 202-606-7828; or online at http://stats.bls.gov/ppihome.htm

Bills, bills, bills

The bond market is where the economy stretches its legs. Find out whether to invest in a T-bill or a T-bird, or whether savings bonds are still great graduation gifts.

The U.S. Department of Treasury will tell you all you need to know about Treasury bills, notes, and bonds, as well as auction results, and more.

Call: Treasury Bills Hotline; 202-874-4000; or online at http://www.treas.gov/

A job bank for globetrotters

Throw out the classifieds. Uncle Sam is always hiring bright people like yourself, not just here but all over the world.

This Career America hotline, sponsored by the U.S. Office of Personnel Management, will help you find out exactly what government jobs are available in your area, what the qualifications are, and to whom you need to talk to get you started on the payroll.

Call: Career America Hotline; 912-757-3000; or online at http://www.usajobs.opm.gov/

Whom do you believe?

Did the product you bought to grow hair on your head actually just color your scalp? Did you buy a "Made In America" product only to find "Made in Taiwan" stamped on the bottom?

The Federal Trade Commission deals with unfair methods of competition and unfair or deceptive acts or practices. You can call this message line for weekly Commission information on topics for meetings, hearings, and speeches.

Call: Federal Trade Commission Meetings Message Line; 202-326-2710; or online at http://www.ftc.gov/

Labor pains

Out of work or looking for a new job? You can take comfort in the numbers while tracking the latest employment trends and opportunities. The U.S. Department of Labor provides information on employment levels, labor indicators, consumer and producer prices as well as information on available publications on this recorded message.

Call: Current Labor Statistics; 202-606-7828; or online at http://stats.bls. gov/oeshome.htm

What comes in goes out

Are you due for a raise? Would you like to know how the whole country is doing? What about wages and salaries? Call to get month by month personal income and outlays, total wages and salaries, proprietors' income, interest and dividend income, and more from the U.S. Department of Commerce.

Call: Personal Income and Outlays Message Line; 202-606-5303; or online at http://www.doc.gov/

Recall their bluff

You can become a grassroots pain in the pocketbook for manufacturers of shoddy products. The U.S. Consumer Product Safety Commission Investigations hotline will tell you how to make your complaints heard and also tell you about available publications and tips on purchasing products.

Call: Consumer Product Safety Commission Hotline; 800-638-CPSC; or online at http://www.cpsc.gov/

An ARM and a leg

Keep a step ahead of the bank if you have an adjustable rate mortgage (ARM) by tracking fluctuation in interest rates. Remember, it's your pound of flesh. Call the Office of Thrift Supervision to hear a recorded message on the current data that is used by many financial institutions as a basis for computing their adjustable rate mortgages.

Call: Office of Thrift Supervision; 202-906-6988; or online at http://www.ots.treas.gov/

Project Blue Book

In 1969 the government undertook a huge investigation of UFO sightings called Project Blue Book.

The case is now closed and all the findings are available to the public at the National Archives on 95 rolls of microfilm containing over 2.3 million pages. They offer a free brochure, fact sheet, and a bibliography. You can also get up to 10 pages of an individual sighting report from the Project copied and sent to you free of charge.

Contact: National Archives and Records Administration, Textual Reference Branch, 8601 Adelphi Rd., College Park, MD 20740-6001; 301-713-7250; or online at http://www.nara.gov/

The latest dirt

Should you plant sunflowers or soybeans? Should you invest in pork bellies or potatoes? Is the local grocery chain inflating its prices? The U.S. Department of Agriculture newsline will tell you more than you ever will need to know. And depending upon when you call, you can also keep up on political appointments and the latest agricultural techniques and discoveries.

Call: Agriculture Department News Hotline; 202-488-8358; or online at http://www.usda.gov/

How much is too much?

Uncle Sam goes shopping each month and you can find out how much we spend on everything from cupcakes to satellite dishes. It's a goldmine for comparison shoppers and entrepreneurs looking for the next supermarket. Call for the latest U.S. Department of Labor figures.

Call: Consumer Price Index; 202-606-7828; or online at http://stats.bls.gov/cpihome.htm

Ready to hit the open road?

This message system of the Office of Personnel Management is set up to provide information to current or retired federal employees or survivors, regarding retirement benefits, forms necessary, as well as directing you to the appropriate sources for more information.

Call: Federal Employees Retirement Information Hotline; 202-606-0500; or online at http://www.opm.gov/retire/index.htm

Your travel agent

Plan ahead for your trip to the nation's Capitol. This message provides you with information on what is happening at the 14 Smithsonian museums, including hours of operation and special exhibits.

Call: Smithsonian Dial-A-Museum; 202-357-2020; or online at http://www.si.edu/

Share the wealth

Tired of sitting back and watching third world countries fall apart before your eyes? You can become a Peace Corps volunteer and use your special talents to improve life.

Call: Peace Corps; 800-424-8580; or online at http://www. peacecorps.gov/

Does money grow on trees?

You can see money being made by the billions during your tour of the Bureau of Engraving and Printing. Call this message line for information concerning tour hours, directions, and best places to park. You shouldn't leave your wallet at home, as they have a great gift shop too.

Call: Engraving and Printing Message Line; 202-874-3188; or online at http://www.bep.treas.gov/

Better than sitting home

Are you retired, and love the outdoors? Want to volunteer? Give some time to the U.S. Geological Survey (USGS). You can get a comprehensive listing of all USGS departments, phone numbers, and division coordinators.

Call: Geological Survey Volunteers Hotline; 703-648-7440; or online at http://www.usgs.gov/

Televidiots, fight back

Tired of being pushed around by the obnoxious cable companies? Mysterious 900 charge on your phone bill?

Don't get mad as heck, get even. File a complaint. You can learn about the process and also get free facts and publications by calling the U.S. Federal Communications Commission Public Service Division.

Call: Federal Communications Commission Public Service Division; 202-418-0190; or online at http://www.fcc.gov/

Let your fingers do the walking

Just sit back, relax, and dial up a job for yourself. The Federal Job Information Center of the Office of Personnel Management can provide you with information on the application process, job availability, testing centers, and more. Just give a call and get your career jumpstarted.

Call: Federal Job Information Center Hotline; 202-606-2700; or online at http://www.usajobs.opm.gov/

Pick a job, any job

Looking for a career with the lowest current unemployment rate? Are your prospects of getting off unemployment improving? Call the U.S. Department of Labor Employment Situation Information recorded message line for current information on the unemployment rate, unemployment rate of major worker groups, and other labor market activity.

Call: Employment Situation Information; 202-606-7828; or online at http://stats.bls.gov/lavhome.htm

A big number for small business

You ask it; they answer it. The U.S. Small Business Administration (SBA) provides you with a wealth of information for all your small business needs, including publications, videos, local SBA offices, referrals, and more.

Call: SBA Answer Desk; 800-8-ASK-SBA; or online at http://www.sba.gov/

Plan ahead

Is your child another Einstein? Then you better start saving now for college. Call the Savings Bond hotline of the U.S. Department of Treasury to receive information on the market base interest rate of bonds, and to find out about the education savings bond program.

Call: Savings Bonds Hotline; 800-4US-BOND; or online at http://www.treas.gov/

Uncle Sam's poor box

Want to help Uncle Sam pay off his charge account? Just call this number sponsored by the U.S. Department of Treasury's Bureau of the Public Debt and hear who you need to make the check out to and do your part.

Call: Public Debt Information Line; 202-874-4000; or online at http://www.publicdebt.treas.gov/

Flower-power plus

Get green-thumb advice from the bonsai samurai staffers at the U.S. Botanic Garden in Washington, DC. Listen to the nation's Gardeners of Eden and learn about free on-site classes for visitors and expert analysis of your own gardening problems by phone.

Call: Botanic Garden Upcoming Events Hotline; 202-225-8333; or online at http://www.aoc.gov/usbg/overview.htm

Stars in your eyes

Are you a star gazer? Want to impress your date with your terrestrial knowledge? Just call the Skywatchers Report to learn what the most prominent stars and planets are in the sky this month, and maybe your date will start gazing into your eyes.

Call: Smithsonian Skywatchers Report; 202-357-2000; or online at http://www.si.edu/

Here's money you didn't know you had

Need a little extra cash to pay the holiday bills?

The IRS may be trying to give you a refund, but can't find you. There are more than 96,000 unclaimed checks worth more than $50 million dollars waiting at the IRS (average check $518).

To find out if one of the checks is yours, call 800-829-1040 and ask. It could be your lucky day. You can also contact the IRS online at http://www.irs.gov/

Cost of illegal drugs

Just how much is the illegal traffic of drugs costing the country? The Drugs and Crime Data Center and Clearinghouse has the most current data on drugs and crime, and will do free searches of their database for you on specific topics.

Contact: Drugs and Crime Data Center and Clearinghouse, 1600 Research Blvd., Rockville, MD 20850; 800-666-3332, or 301-251-5140 (in DC metro area); or online at http://www.ojp.usdoj.gov/bjs/

A raise is a raise

By any other name, it still smells sweet. You can find out if everyone's getting a raise but you. Or, if your benefits are keeping up with the Joneses.

Call the Employment Cost Index Information recorded message at the U.S. Department of Labor; 202-606-7828; or online at http://stats.bls.gov/ecthome.htm

Aye and nay

Have your senators been busy? Just give a call to see what they've been doing. This message provides you with information regarding when the Senate was in session, bills voted on, and their outcomes.

Call: U.S. Senate Floor Votes: Democratic Cloakroom; 202-224-8541. Republican Cloakroom; 202-224-8601; or online at http://www.senate.gov

Tally up

Want to know how your guy voted? Have you been following a particular bill? This message provides you with information regarding when the House was in session, bills voted on, and their outcomes.

Call: U.S. House of Representatives Floor Votes: Democratic Cloakroom; 202-225-7400. Republican Cloakroom; 202-225-7430; or online at http://www.house.gov/

Loose lips save ships

No need to stay on a sinking ship if you plan ahead. Call for information on boating safety recalls, consumer complaints about boat defects, and even boating classes.

Call: Boating Safety Hotline; 800-368-5647; or online at http://www.uscg.mil/

Cancer answers

Each day the newspaper seems to carry a story on a new cancer treatment, cure, or prevention method. What do you believe?

The Cancer Information Service is the place to call for the latest information on detection, treatment, rehab, and financial assistance for those concerned about cancer.

Call: Cancer Information Service; 800-4-CANCER; or online at http://rex.nci.nih.gov/

Television interference problems

Is your favorite TV show ruined by interference from a local radio station? Does your cordless phone pick up radio signals?

The Interference Handbook is a free publication from the Federal Communications Commission (FCC) on your interference problems.

Contact: Consumer Assistance, Federal Communications Commission, 1919 M St., NW, Room 725, Washington, DC 20554; 202-418-0200; or online at http://www.fcc.gov/

Legal or not?

Is getting your green card turning you red? The Immigration and Naturalization Service has set up a message line to provide information on forms, nearest offices, passports, green cards, citizenship, work visas, foreign adoption, bringing your family to the U.S., and more.

Call: Immigration and Naturalization Message Line; 800-375-5283; or online at http://www.ins.usdoj.gov/index.html

April 15th seems to come earlier each year

The Internal Revenue Service has the hottest lines in town. Their Information Line answers all your tax questions. Their Tele-Tax Line provides pre-recorded tax information. And the Forms Line will send you those special tax forms we all love.

Call: Information Line; 800-829-1040, Tele-Tax Line; 800-829-4477, Forms Line; 800-829-3676; or online at http://www.irs.gov/

Social Security: Just another wrong number?

Everyone complains about how little they get each month from Social Security, but if their check is late, look out.

Need to get another copy of your Social Security card? Moved? Want to know how much you will get from Social Security if you retired today? Just give this hotline a call, and don't forget your special number.

Call: Social Security Hotline; 800-772-1213; or online at http://www.ssa.gov/

The economic outlook

The Congressional Budget Office has a report available called *The Economic and Budget Outlook* which is an analysis of the economic outlook.

Information included are projections of the Federal deficit and debt by fiscal year developments in the labor market and much more.

For your copy contact: Congressional Budget Office, Second and D St., SW, Washington, DC 20515; 202-226-2809; or online at http://www.cbo.gov/

UFOs

Where do you get information on Unidentified Flying Objects (UFOs)? The Air Force will send you a free UFO Fact Sheet that lists key resources, both government and private, to get you started in your search for extraterrestrial life.

Contact: U.S. Air Force, Office of Public Affairs, Resource Library, 1690 Air Force Pentagon, Washington, DC 20330-1690; 703-697-4100; or online at http://www.af.mil/

Disappearing towns

Your map is brand new, but you can't find the town where your grandmother says she was born. Before you write your grandmother off as crazy, there's free help.

The U.S. Geological Survey can search its Geographic Names database for you to find out if it still exists, or if it doesn't, the exact longitude and latitude of where it used to be.

Contact: Geographic Names Information, Branch of Geographic Names, U.S. Geologic Survey, 12201 Sunrise Valley Dr., Mail Stop 523, Reston, VA 22092; 800-872-6277; or online at http://mapping.usgs.gov/www/gnis/

Environmentalists unite

INFOTERRA, a part of the Environmental Protection Agency, offers a free information exchange network connected with the United Nations. It can keep you up to date on the latest in environmental rules, regulations, and developments, and can serve as a clearinghouse for activists to exchange ideas. Files on the system will soon include pictures, sounds, videos, and software.

Many of INFOTERRA's files are available on Internet. To learn more about INFOTERRA, contact 202-260-5917 (voice); or online at http://www.unep.org/unep/eia/ein/infoterr/

Medicare madness...keep tabs on benefit erosion

How do you apply for Medicare benefits? What is and is not covered? What about supplemental insurance?

The Medicare Hotline will help you maneuver through the forms and filing maze to get what you deserve.

Call: Medicare Hotline; 800-638-6833; or online at http://www.hcfa. gov/medicare/mcarensm.htm

Don't be a broke bookworm

Money's tight everywhere, but Uncle Sam can help you pay for school. The Federal Student Aid Information Center can help would-be college and trade school students learn about financial aid programs, understand eligibility requirements and even complete financial aid applications.

Call: Federal Student Aid Information Center; 800-4-FED-AID; or online at http://www.ed.gov/offices/ope/students/

When meat's a mystery, call Uncle Sam

Worried about that special recipe Uncle Bob has for cooking the Thanksgiving bird? What about the smoked turkey your grandma sent through the mail? The Meat and Poultry Hotline answers questions related to food safety, preparation tips, power failures, and food labels.

Call: Meat and Poultry Hotline; 800-535-4555; or online at http://www.usda.gov/agency/fsis/homepage.htm

Understanding lemons, roadkills, grouchy drivers

Learn about safety problems in motor vehicles, tires, and automotive equipment. Get even with your manufacturer by having the defective product recalled. If a safety-related defect exists, the manufacturer has to fix it at no cost to the owner.

Call: Auto Safety Hotline; 888-327-4236; or online at http://www.nhtsa.dot.gov/hotline/hotline.html

The dump snitchline

Does your dump have a very funny odor? Want to start recycling? Wondering what can be dumped in your dump?

The Resource Conservation and Recovery Act (RCRA)/Superfund Hotline will answer these questions and more, including hazardous waste disposal, used oil, and land disposal restrictions.

Call: RCRA/Superfund Hotline; 800-424-9346; or online at http://www.epa.gov/superfund/

Spreading the clean (and sober) word

Are drugs or alcohol taking over your life? What about someone you love? Want to help keep your kids off drugs? Call this number and receive publications, posters, videos, and even treatment and referral information.

Call: National Clearinghouse for Alcohol and Drug Information; 800-729-6686; or online at http://www.health.org/

The rich get richer, the poor get poorer

Feel like you never get ahead? According to the Census Bureau, this seems to be true. The *Current Population Report, Income, Poverty, Wealth in the U.S.* ($4.25 s/n 803-005-30026-9), is full of tables, charts, and graphs to show you who is getting ahead and who is lagging behind.

For ordering information contact: Bureau of the Census, U.S. Department of Commerce, Federal Office Building 3, Silver Hill and Suitland Roads, Suitland, MD 20746, 301-457-4100; or online at http://www.census.gov/

Who contributed to whom

Want to know who your boss supported in the last election? What about the local judge or councilman?

You can get a listing of all the federal campaigns and to whom a person contributed funds just by submitting a request to the Federal Election Commission. They can conduct a free search that goes back to 1980. You can even see how much the president gave before he was elected.

For more information contact: Public Records Office, Federal Election Commission, 999 E St., NW, Washington, DC 20463; 800-424-9530, 202-219-3420 (DC), 202-219-3336 (TTY).

Confessed under hypnosis?

Did the police make you confess to a crime you didn't commit because they put you under hypnosis? Find out how they did it, and how valid confessions obtained under hypnosis are in the courtroom, from the free publication, *Forensic Use of Hypnosis*.

Contact: Office for Victims of Crime Resource Center, Box 6000-AIQ, Rockville, MD 20850; 800-627-6872.

Get a picture from above

If it's in the U.S., the U.S. Geological Survey (USGS) has a picture. You can get a photograph of your neighborhood through the Aerial Photography Program, with most photographs showing a ground area of about 5x5 miles. Prices start at $6.

For more information contact: Customer User Services, EROS, U.S. Geological Survey, Mundt Federal Bldg. Sioux Falls, SD 57198; 605-594-6511; or online at http://edcwww.cr.usgs.gov/webglis

The safe sex buzz

You can find out the latest information on AIDS, such as locations of testing centers near you, treatment and referral options, and answers to questions like, can you get AIDS if you use a condom?

Call: The Centers for Disease Control-National AIDS Hotline; 800-342-AIDS; or online at http://www.ashastd.org/nah/nah.html

For your nonprofit

# Chapter 17

For your nonprofit

Tons of free books

Need to raise a little cash? Hold a book sale.

Thousands of surplus books from the Copyright Division and private gifts in a variety of subject areas are available to non-profit organizations from the Library of Congress.

All you need is a letter from your non-profit organization which includes the name of the person coming to select books and the name of the organization, but you must pay for shipping and handling.

Or you can bring a letter from your Congressman's office. Their office will have the option of paying for the shipping with franks (postage for which their office will pay).

Contact: Surplus Books Program, Anglo-American Acquisitions Division, Library of Congress, Madison Bldg., 101 Independence Ave., SE, Room B03, Washington, DC 20540; 202-707-9514; or online at http://leweb.loc. gov/acq/surplus.html

Learn the ropes

Don't let the IRS rain on your parade. Get all your ducks in a row before there are any unpleasant surprises.

Contact the Internal Revenue Service for a guidebook *Tax-Exempt Status For Your Organization* (Publication 557) on tax-exempt nonprofits. It explains the procedures you must follow to obtain an appropriate ruling or a determination letter recognizing such exemption, as well as certain other information that applies generally to all exempt organizations.

Contact: The Internal Revenue Service Forms Line; 800-829-3676; or online at http://www.irs.gov/

Giveaway wish list

Need some desks, chairs, even hospital beds for your nonprofit? Nonprofits, which include medical institutions, clinics, schools, museums, libraries and more, can receive free furniture, clothing, and equipment from Uncle Sam through their state surplus property agency, which receives items for distribution from the federal government.

To find out about the office near you, request the brochure *Federal Surplus Personal Property Donation Programs* from Property Management, Federal Supply Service, General Services Administration, Washington, DC 20406; 703-305-7240; or online at http://www.fss.gsa.gov/property.html

Step inside the loop

So who's getting all that money Congress spends each year in grants?

Find out in a free Congressional Research Service report *Grants And Foundation Support* (IP50G), which helps the grantseeker find sources of funding, both government and private, and grant proposal development.

Request the publication through your congressman's office, U.S. Congress, Washington, DC 20515; 202-224-3121; or online at http://www.house. gov/berman/97-67.htm

Strike up the band

Your parade can get a little noisier and more colorful with a band and color guard supplied by some local Defense Department installations.

Most installations have community relations officers who handle requests from nonprofit organizations for these services and more, so contact them for information on availability and restrictions.

If you would like an aerial flyover from the Blue Angels or the Thunderbirds, or a parachute show from the Golden Knights (there are some costs involved), contact: OASD (PA) DCR, The Pentagon, Room 1E776, Washington, DC 20301-1400; 703-614-6543. The request must be put in writing on Department of Defense Form #DD2535, which can be found online at:

http://web1.whs.osd.mil/forms/dd2535.pdf

A home for the holidays

If you are part of a non-profit organization ministering to the homeless, the government is taking applications for eligible groups to receive excess or unused federal buildings or land for homeless people.

The program is administered by a combination of the U.S. Department of Housing and Urban Development (HUD), which screens applications, the General Services Administration (GSA), which makes the properties available, and the U.S. Department of Health and Human Services (HHS), which reviews applications. In accordance with Title V of the McKinney Homeless Assistance Act, HUD publishes a list of properties available in the Federal Register.

Additional information regarding the properties, as well as the Title V process can be obtained by calling 800-927-7588, a toll-free number established by HUD. After a property is published, homeless providers must submit expressions of interest by providing a written notice to the Division of Health Facilities Planning at HHS within 60 days of publication. You will then receive an application packet containing complete instructions on how to apply for the property.

You can also request the following publications: *How To Acquire Federal Surplus Real Property for Public Health Purposes, Obtaining Federal Property for the Homeless, Questions and Answers About Federal Property Programs,* and *HHS/HUD/GSA joint regulation* covering specific information on Title V process.

Contact: Division of Property Management, Program Support Center, U.S. Department of Health and Human Services, Room 5B-41, Parklawn Building, 5600 Fishers Lane, Rockville, MD 20857; 301-443-2265; or online at http://aspe.os.dhhs.gov/96cfda/p93291.htm

Soup's on

Does your nonprofit offer meals or food to those in need? Through the Food Distribution Program, the U.S. Department of Agriculture (USDA) distributes foods to state agencies for use by eligible local agencies.

USDA purchases foods from U.S. markets under surplus removal and price support programs. The foods go to schools and institutions participating in the child nutrition programs, to nutrition programs for the elderly, to needy families on Indian reservations, and to food banks, soup kitchens, hospitals, and prisons.

The foods are also used to help victims of natural disasters and situations of distress. For a free copy of *Food Distribution—State Distributing Agencies Directory*, contact the address listed below.

Contact: Food Distribution Division, Food and Nutrition Service, U.S. Department of Agriculture, 3101 Park Ctr. Dr., Room 502, Alexandria, VA 22302; 703-305-2680; or online at http://www.usda.gov/fcs/food.htm

Pledge drive propaganda

Overcome contribution jitters by handing out a copy of Publication 526 titled *Charitable Contributions*, which explains the contributions you can deduct and the types of organizations that qualify.

Contact: The Internal Revenue Service Forms Line, 800-829-3676; or online at http://www.irs.gov/

For your pets

18

Chapter 18

For your pets

And you thought they were just cute

They are more than Snoopy's cousins; beagles have now been put to work. USDA's *Beagle Brigade* is a free coloring book which explains the background, training, care and feeding of a group of detector dogs that work in international airports throughout the United States keeping a lookout for agricultural contraband. A number of free postcards and fact sheets are available including *Beagle Trivia*, which provides information on the origin, characteristics, and myths about beagles.

Contact: Animal and Plant Health Inspection Service, U.S. Department of Agriculture (USDA), 4700 River Road, Unit 51, Riverdale, MD 20737; 301-734-7799; or online at http://www.aphis.usda.gov/

It was love at first sight

You were strolling along an idyllic river in France when you stumbled upon an injured ferret. You nursed it back to health and now you want to bring it home with you.

Pets and Wildlife is a free publication that describes the rules regarding bringing pets and wildlife into the U.S., and the quarantine procedures, as well as a list of prohibited species.

For your free copy write: U.S. Customs Service, P.O. Box 7407, Washington, DC 20044; call 317-290-3149; or online at http://www.customs.treas.gov/travel/pets.htm

Mommy, Mommy, may I PLEASE have a dog?

Kids beg their parents every day for a family pet, but few know what is involved, such as the care and feeding of a household pet.

The office below has several fact sheets which parents can use to teach their children how to care for pets properly.

Some of the free fact sheets include:

- *Dog Ownership Self-Test*— for people who are considering adopting a dog

- *Care and Nurturing of Cats*—which provides information on your cat's health.

The office also has two free publications dealing with pet food:

- *Information on Marketing a Pet Food Product*

- *Selecting Nutritious Pet Foods*

Contact: Center for Veterinary Medicine, Food and Drug Administration, 7500 Standish Place, HFV-12, Rockville, MD 20855; 301-594-1755; or online at http://www.cvm.fda.gov/

Take good care of Fido

Do you run an animal lab or breeding enterprise and want to train your staff? What about animal husbandry? The Animal Welfare Information Center has a free publication *Audio-Visuals Relating to Animal Care, Use, and Welfare*, which lists videos they have available for free interlibrary loan. These videos cover topics such as livestock, household pets, lab animals, rabbits, guinea pigs, husbandry, and more.

For your copy contact: Animal Welfare Information Center, National Agricultural Library, 10301 Baltimore Blvd., 5th Floor, Beltsville, MD 20705; 301-504-6212; or online at http://netvet.wustl.edu/awic.htm

For your pleasure

Chapter 19

For your pleasure

Turn on the ocean blue

Change the channel from "Bowling for Dollars" to a wonderful film or video on fish and wildlife, which are available for free loan through the Fish and Wildlife Service regional offices. Some of the topic areas covered include current research and environmental issues, wetland, fisheries and more, and several even come with teacher's guides. Here is a sampling of the more popular videos:

- "America's Wetlands"

- "A Home For Pearl"

- "In Celebration of America's Wildlife"

- "Parrots of Luquillo"

- "Striper! Restoring Coastal Striped Bass"

Contact your regional office for more information, or you may contact the Office of Public Affairs for information regarding the office nearest you: Office of Public Affairs,

Fish and Wildlife Service, U.S. Department of Interior, Washington DC 20240; 202-208-5611; or online at http://www.fws.gov/

Outer space in Omaha

Actually, the National Aeronautics and Space Administration (NASA), through the Aerospace Education Services Program, will send people anywhere in the U.S. to discuss NASA history, rocketry, living and working in space, aeronautics, and more. They can conduct assemblies, classroom visits, teachers' workshops, and hands-on activities. The visits are scheduled by ten NASA field centers.

To find a field center near you, contact the NASA Dryden Flight Research Center, P.O. Box 273, MS 4839A, NASA, Edwards, CA 93523; 805-258-2445; or online at http://trc.dfrc.nasa.gov/teacher/aesp.html

News of the day

Remember when newsreels were shown at the movies? Those same newsreels are available for viewing through the National Archives.

The Universal Newsreels cover the period between 1929—1967. Like other newsreels, these appeared semi-weekly at theaters, averaging ten minutes per issue. You can view the newsreels at the Archives, or you can pay a nominal fee to a service to have them make a special copy for you. Find out what exciting things were happening in the world on the day you were born!

Contact: Motion Picture, Sound, and Video Branch, National Archives, 8601 Adelphi Rd., College Park, MD 20740; 301-713-7060; or online at http://www.nara.gov/nara/nn/nns/nnsm.html

Some enchanted evening

Enjoy a nice romantic afternoon or evening listening to the concert of your choice. This is not just a summer affair, but year round! Most performances are in the Washington area. However, there are other performances along the East Coast. Don't miss out. Information is available through each of the Armed Forces bands.

Air Force Band, 23 Mill St., Bolling Air Force Base, Washington, DC 20032; 202-767-4310, 202-767-5658 (recorded information line).

Navy Band, Washington Navy Yard, Building 105, Washington, DC 20032; 202-433-2394, 202-433-2525 (recorded information line).

Marine Band, 8th and I St., SW, Washington, DC 20390; 202-433-5809, 202-433-4011 (recorded information line).

Army Band, Building 400, Fort Myers, VA 22211; 703-696-3718, 703-696-3399 (recorded information line).

Yodeling cowboys

From Woody Guthrie to Woody Woodpecker, Indonesian temple gongs to roots gospel, the Folkway Records Archive is likely to have something to get you dancing. And if you ain't got rhythm, they also have plenty of spoken word recordings of historical figures and events. Even the soothing sounds of machines at work. There is a minimal cost for all recordings.

For a free catalogue contact: Folkways Records Archive, Center For Folklife Programs and Cultural Studies, 955 L'Enfant Plaza, SW, Suite 2600, Washington, DC 20560; 202-287-3424; or online at http://www.si.edu/folklife/

Sound bites from history

Want to hear Amelia Earhart talking about the future of flight? Or Thomas Edison talking about the future of electricity?

You can hear famous speeches by past presidents, Supreme Court oral arguments, NASA recordings of air to ground communications, and even National Public Radio broadcasts. There are more than 160,000 sound recordings to choose from! All you need to do is start compiling a list.

You can go to the National Archives and make copies for free, or there are service providers who will make copies for you for a fee.

For more information, contact: Motion Picture, Sound, and Video Branch, National Archives, 8601 Adelphi Rd., College Park, MD 20740; 301-713-7060; or online at http://www.nara.gov/nara/nn/nns/nnsm.html

Science and you

The National Science Foundation (NSF) produces a limited number of films and videos each year to report the progress of scientific research and its applications to the public. A few of these productions document research results for a more narrowly focused, technical audience. All of them reflect important research and cover a large array of scientific disciplines supported by the Foundation.

NSF audiovisuals are available directly from the distributors and information is provided on the types of services offered (rental/sale/free loan).

For your free *Film and Video Catalog* (NSF-97-122), contact: National Science Foundation Office of Public Affairs, 4201 Wilson Boulevard, Room 1245, Arlington, VA 22230; 301-947-2722; or online at http://www.nsf.gov/

The latest technologies

The National Institute of Standards and Technology (NIST) is a major source of technical expertise for U.S. businesses seeking to use the latest technologies to improve their products and processes. A number of the NIST's programs are featured in videotapes and are available for interlibrary loan. Some of the titles include:

- "The Fun and Excitement of Invention"

- "Quest For Excellence V"

- "Mexico Earthquake"

For a free catalogue contact: Audiovisual Communications, Public Affairs Division, A903 Administration Building, National Institute of Standards and Technology, Gaithersburg, MD 20899; 301-975-3058; or online at http://www.nist.gov/

Star Wars speaker

The U.S. Department of Defense will send a speaker almost anywhere in the country to speak on Star Wars, MIAs/POWs, or many other current events. Your social group, school, or just a group of interested people can learn more about Defense Department topics simply by contacting the Speakers Bureau 6 to 8 weeks in advance. Some travel expenses may be required.

For more information, contact the Public Affairs Office of your local military installation, or: OASD Speakers Bureau, Public Affairs, Directorate for Community Relations, Pentagon, Room 1E776, Washington, DC 20301; 703-695-3845.

Banking on screen

The Federal Reserve Bank offers a variety of films, filmstrips, and videos available for free loan through your regional Federal Reserve Bank. The topics covered include the monetary system, electronic funds transfer, free enterprise, and the history of money.

Some of the titles available include:

- "Both Borrower and Lender"

- "The Fed: Our Central Bank"

- "To Your Credit"

- "Money: Summing It Up"

- "Too Much, Too Little"

For a publications catalogue and lending information contact: Federal Reserve Bank of Chicago's Public Information Center, P.O. Box 834, Chicago, IL 60690; 312-322-5111; or online at http://www.frbchi.org/

For your pocketbook

20

Chapter 20

For your pocketbook

America's most wanted

Recognize your neighbor among the mug shots at the post office?

You could be in line for a reward. The Federal Bureau of Investigation (FBI) sometimes pays cold cash for information which leads to an arrest and conviction. All rewards are given on a case by case and cash on delivery basis.

To discuss the specifics, contact: Your local FBI office or Federal Bureau of Investigation, J.E.H. Building, 10th and Pennsylvania Ave., NW, Washington, DC 20535; 202-324-3000; or online at http://www.fbi.gov/

Ton 'o trash ahoy

The next time you take a cruise, don't forget your video camera. Several resourceful cruise takers have caught ship employees dumping large amounts of trash into the ocean, and have won big bucks in court. If you witness or produce evidence of illegal ocean dumping, report it to the Coast Guard. If the case goes to trial and is won, you can receive 50 percent of the penalty assessed.

For more information contact: Marine Environmental Protection Division, U.S. Coast Guard, 2100 2nd St., SW, Washington, DC 20593; or call the National Response Center at 202-267-2675 (DC), 800-424-8802; or online at http://www.uscg.mil/hg/g-m/gmhome.htm

Mother Nature's watchdogs

You can become the first environmental vigilante on your block and get paid by the U.S. Environmental Protection Agency (EPA) for every littering creep you nab.

The Comprehensive Environmental Response Compensation and Liability Act authorizes the EPA at its discretion to pay up to $10,000 for information leading to the arrest and conviction of persons who engage in unreported dumping of hazardous substances.

For more information contact: U.S. Environmental Protection Agency, Criminal Investigation Division, 401 M St., SW, 2232, Washington, DC 20460; 202-564-2490; or online at http://es.eps.gov/oeca

Don't get mad, get even

If you suspect someone is cheating on taxes, tell the Internal Revenue Service (IRS) and receive 10 percent of every dime in back taxes the feds collect. As with everything with the IRS, you must fill out the appropriate form in order to be eligible. Request Form 211, Application For Reward For Original Information.

Call: The Internal Revenue Service; 800-829-3676; or contact them online at http://www.irs.gov/

Mileage meter mess

If you suspect someone's monkeyed with the mileage on that second-hand station wagon you just bought, it's time to squeal. As a victim, you can receive an award up to $1500 or three times the amount of damages, whichever is greater, plus court costs and reasonable attorney fees. The state attorney may even bring civil actions on behalf of consumers.

For more information contact: Auto Safety Hotline, National Highway Traffic Safety Administration, NEF-20, 400 Seventh St., SW Washington, DC 20590; 800-424-9393, 888-327-4236; or online at http://www.nhtsa.dot.gov/hotline/hotline.html

And that $60,000 toilet

Sometimes it seems like there just isn't enough golden fleece to go around. If you know of a case of obvious contractor fraud, you might be eligible for 15-25 percent of the money recovered. You can file a complaint in the U.S. District Courts using the Qui Tam Provisions of the False Claims Act. Your complaint will remain sealed for 60 days during which time the government will investigate to determine if they wish to take over your case. Even if they don't take your case, you can still take your case to trial and if you win you are still eligible for the 15-25 percent.

For more information contact: U.S. Department of Justice, Office of Public Affairs, 10th and Constitution Ave., NW, Washington, DC 20530; 202-514-2000; or online at http://www.usdoj.gov

Bowling for drug kingpins

If suspicious boats, low flying aircraft, even strange activity at the neighbors makes you think that drug activity is taking place, you should report it to your local Drug Enforcement Administration. They give rewards on a case by case basis for information leading to the arrest of individuals involved in drug-related crimes.

For more information contact: The Drug Enforcement Administration field division in your area, or to locate that office, contact Office of Public Affairs, Drug Enforcement Administration, 700 Army-Navy Drive, Arlington, VA 22202; 202-307-7977; or online at http://www.usdoj.gov/dea/

Me and my bogus Kalvins

If you're streetwise, you know what most vendors already know: there's more money in counterfeit bluejeans than in greenbacks. From fake Gucci bags to phony Pac-Man cassettes, the Customs Service will pay for bonafide tips. They pay rewards to people who provide Customs with original information which results in a seizure, arrest, or indictment, with a maximum reward of $2500.

Contact: U.S. Customs Service, 1301 Constitution Ave., NW, Washington, DC 20229; 800-BE-ALERT; or online at http://www.customs.treas.gov/

Double-dipping doctors

If you can figure out your Medicare bill, you may find some charges that don't make sense. Take the time to look a little deeper, and if you discover some instances of Medicare fraud, file your complaint with the U.S. District Courts using the Qui Tam Provisions of the False Claims Act. The U.S. Department of

Justice will investigate, and if they take the case and win, you can receive 15-25 percent of the money.

For more information contact: U.S. Department of Justice, 10th and Constitution Ave., NW, Washington, DC 20530; 202-514-2000; or online at http://www.usdoj.gov/

A smuggler's loss is your gain

Cessna airplanes, snazzy automobiles, jewelry, liquor, real estate, boats, and exotic birds are some of the items seized by the U.S. Customs agents from people trying to bring products illegally into the country. These items are auctioned off all over the U.S.

For information on auctions contact:
EG&G Dynatrend, U.S. Customs Support Division, 3702 Pender Dr., Suite 400, Fairfax, VA 22030; 703-273-3441; or online at http://www.customs.ustreas.gov/

Free mugger's money

The Victims of Crime Act of 1984 created a Crime Victims Fund in the U.S. Treasury to provide federal financial assistance to state governments to compensate and assist victims of crime. Victims are compensated for expenses such as medical costs resulting from victimization. To get additional information you should contact your local police department or the Office of Justice Programs.

Contact: Office of Congressional and Public Affairs, Office of Justice Programs, U.S. Department of Justice, 633 Indiana Ave., NW, Washington, DC 20531; 202-307-0781; or online at http://www.ojp.usdoj.gov/ovc

Taking advantage of defense downsizing

The only government agency that is really shrinking is Defense. This means that it will be getting rid of more stuff than ever before. Tents, sporting equipment, computers, horses, furniture, telephone systems, photographic equipment, and even entire military bases.

The merchandise is sold at over 200 locations worldwide. Information on local and national sales is available in the free booklet *How To Buy Surplus Personal Property From DOD*. To obtain your booklet contact: Defense Reutilization and Marketing Service, International Sales Office, P.O. Box 5275 DDRC, 2163 Airways Blvd., Memphis, TN 38114; 800-GOVT-BUY; or online at http://www.pueblo.gsa.gov/cic_text/fed_prog/other/persprop.txt

For your retirement

Chapter 21

For your retirement

Pension central

The Pension Benefit Guaranty Corporation monitors most private sector-defined benefit plans that provide a benefit based on factors such as age, years of service, and average or highest salary. They have the following free publications:

- *Employer's Pension Guide*—provides a general overview of the responsibilities under federal law of employers who sponsor single-employer defined benefit pension plans.

- *Your Guaranteed Pension*—answers some of the most frequently asked questions about the Pension Benefit Guaranty Corporation and its termination insurance program for single-employer defined benefit pension plans.

- *Your Pension: Things You Should Know About Your Pension Plan*— serves as an explanation of pension plans; what they are, how they operate, and the rights and options of participants.

Contact: Public Affairs, Pension Benefit Guaranty Corporation, 1200 K Street, NW, Suite 240, Washington, DC 20005; 202-326-4040; or online at http://www.pbgc.gov

Social insecurity

It's not enough you'll have to worry about your dentures slipping, but you might have to live on cat food, too.

The Social Security system will be in ruins and inflation will have rendered your pension laughable. What's a frightened taxpayer to do?

Request a free *Personal Earnings and Benefit Statement*. It includes a complete work history statement, outlining how much you will receive at age 62, as well as how much you would receive on disability or for your survivors.

You can request a form from Social Security by calling 800-772-1213; or online at http://www.ssa.gov

Don't let yourself become a victim

Retirement is supposed to be a time of relaxation and enjoyment. But you must take some measures to protect yourself from unscrupulous thugs. *Elderly Victims* is a free report which outlines some problem areas, and steps you can take to avoid becoming another victim.

Contact: National Institute of Justice, NCJRS, Box 6000, Department AID, Rockville, MD 20850; 800-851-3420, 301-251-5500; or online at http://www.ncjrs.org

Pensions—an investment for your future

Don't assume your pension is a sure thing. Make sure it is safe and secure. The Pension and Welfare Benefits Administration helps to protect the retirement security of working Americans through the Employment Retirement Income Security Act.

They require administrators of private pension and welfare plans to provide plan participants with easily understandable summaries of plans, to file those summaries with the agency; and to report annually on the financial operation of the plans and bonding of persons charged with handling plan funds and assets.

They have many free publications dealing with pension plans including: *What You Should Know About Your Pension Rights*—which gives a summary of what is required of pension plans, and *How To File A Claim For Your Benefit*—which explains what you need to do to receive your benefit.

Contact: Division of Public Information, Pension and Welfare Benefits Administration, U.S. Department of Labor, 200 Constitution Ave., NW, Room N5656, Washington, DC 20210; 202-219-8921, 800-998-7542 (publications only); or online at http://www.dol.gov/dol/pwba

For your soul

Chapter 22

For your soul

For that special day

The president doesn't want to miss a good party. He can only be so many places at once, but he will at least remember those special occasions such as graduations, weddings, and retirement with a special note. It is important to give enough notice in order to make sure cards arrive on time.

Contact: White House, Greetings Office, 1600 Pennsylvania Ave., NW, Washington, DC 20500; Fax: 202-456-2806; or online at http://www.whitehouse.gov/

Against your conscience

Once you hit 18, all males need to head to the post office to register for Selective Service. But what if you have some moral objection to the military or to war?

The Selective Service System provides free fact sheets which contain information on certain aspects of the Selective Service System, including a publication, *Information for Registrants*, which explains who can qualify and what type of service you need to complete.

For this publication or other on Selective Service contact: Public Affairs, Selective Service System, 1515 Wilson Boulevard, 4th Floor, Arlington, VA 22209; 703-605-4100; or online at http://www.sss.gov/

Need a pick-me-up

How about a get well card from the president? All serious illnesses will be acknowledged after being notified by mail or through a fax. Remember, this is for serious illnesses, not the common cold. Also, a sympathy card can mean a lot to someone who has suffered a loss. Let the President send a note of condolence.

Contact: White House, Greetings Office, 1600 Pennsylvania Ave., NW, Washington, DC 20500; Fax: 202-456-2806; or online at http://www.whitehouse.gov

Testimony to service

The Presidential Memorial Certificate is available to the families of honorably discharged, deceased service members or veterans. This certificate is an acknowledgment of a special contribution. To order your certificate, a date of birth, death, and service number or social security number is needed.

Contact: Your regional Veterans Affairs office to order it, or U.S. Department of Veterans Affairs, 941 North Capitol St., NE, Washington, DC 20421; 800-827-1000; or online at http://www.va.gov/cemetery/presmen.htm

Stars and stripes

A flag is available to the families of deceased veterans who were honorably discharged and served during a war period. Requests should be made through the funeral home; however if this does not happen you can make a request within three years of the death.

Contact: U.S. Department of Veterans Affairs, 941 North Capitol St., NE, Washington, DC 20421; 800-827-1000; or online at http://www.va.gov/

Volunteer service

Pictures and stories about disasters and trouble overseas at times rallies communities and individuals into service. Investigate the relief agencies a little before you sign on board.

Voluntary Foreign Aid Programs: Report of American Voluntary Agencies Engaged in Overseas Relief and Development Registered with the Agency for International Development (AID) describes the general nature of the work being carried out by private and voluntary organizations (PVOs) which are registered with AID.

Included is such information as a PVO's geographic focus and sectorial concentration, as well as summaries of support, revenue, and expenditures. For your free copy contact: Private and Voluntary Humanitarian Response, U.S. Agency for International Development, Washington, DC 20523-0804; 202-712-4810; or online at http://www.info.usaid.gov/

Disabled—act on your rights!

Over 43 million Americans share one or more physical or mental disabilities. In order to provide a clear and comprehensive national mandate for the elimination of discrimination against individuals with disabilities, the American With Disabilities Act of 1990 was enacted. To get the specifics of this bill or any bill, write to your senator or congressman or directly to the Document Room.

Contact: Document Room, Hart Building, Washington, DC 20510; or House of Representatives, Document Room, Washington, DC 20515; 202-224-3121; or online at http://www.house.gov or http://www.senate.gov

A new set of wheels

Is it time to retire your old car, and look into a replacement? The Federal Trade Commission (FTC) has a series of publications to help you learn your rights, and provide tips and other information to help you with your search.

- *Consumer Alert! Look Before You Lease* explains car leasing in easy to understand terms.

- *Renting a Car* explains those confusing rental agreements and insurance deals.

- *Car Ads: Reading Between the Lines* explains in easy to understand terms about car financing.

For your free copies, contact: Public Reference, Room 130, Federal Trade Commission, 6th and Pennsylvania Ave., NW, Washington, DC 20580-0001; 202-326-2222; or online at http://www.ftc.gov/

Home shopping

There are many reputable companies out there selling every type of merchandise imaginable over the phone or through the mail. But from time to time, problems do arise.

The Federal Trade Commission (FTC) receives complaints concerning problems with doing businesses by phone. The FTC also has several publications to help you resolve complaints, avoid scams, and more. Some of the titles include:

- *Solving Consumer Problems*

- *Straight Talk About Telemarketing*

- *Prize Offers*

- *Are You a Target of ...Telephone Scams?*

For your free copies contact: Public Reference, Room 130, Federal Trade Commission, 6th and Pennsylvania Ave., NW, Washington, DC 20580; 202-326-2222; or online at http://www.ftc.gov

Don't panic, take leave

The Family and Medical Leave Act of 1993 (PL 103-3) entitles an eligible employee to a total of 12 work weeks of leave during any 12 month period for any of the following reasons: 1) birth, 2) adoption, 3) serious health condition of family member, and 4) serious health condition of employee.

To find out additional information and to get a copy of the bill, write your senator or congressman or write directly to the Document Room.

Contact: Document Room, Hart Building, Washington, DC 20510; or House of Representatives, Document Room, Washington, DC 20515; 202-224-3121; or online at http://www.house.gov/ or http://www.senate.gov/

Where did you begin?

Where to Write for Vital Records: Births, Deaths, Marriages, and Divorces ($2.25) provides information about the availability of individual vital records maintained on file in state or local vital statistics offices.

It includes a list of vital statistics offices for every state or locale, their addresses, estimated costs, and remarks for each type of record.

For your copy contact: Superintendent of Documents, U.S. Government Printing Office, Washington, DC 20402; 202-512-1800; or online at http://www.gpo.gov/

A flag honoring a special day

Why not commemorate your family's special day with an American flag? It could be the day someone was discharged from the service, an anniversary, or even the birth of a child.

Flags can be purchased through your congressman's office and cost between $14.05-$23. Each flag comes with a certificate stating the day the flag was flown over the Capitol.

For more information contact: Your senator or representative, The Capitol, Washington, DC 20510; 202-224-3121; or online at http://www. senate.gov or http://www.house.gov

Generations: A universal family album

For many people, there are few things more treasured than their children's first shoes. The Smithsonian Traveling Exhibition Service (SITES) produces posters related to exhibitions.

"Generations" is a photograph of a newborn's feet inset among a dozen pairs of baby shoes from various cultures and time periods which commemorates the inaugural exhibition of the Smithsonian's International Gallery. (25" x 21", $5 + $4 s/h per order).

Contact: SITES, Publications Department 0564, Washington, DC 20073-0564; 202-357-3168, ext. 117; or online at http://www.si.edu

International peace

The purpose of the United Nations (UN) is not just international peace and security but also to develop friendly relations among nations.

There are many publications available about the UN and its accomplishments, including *Charter of the United Nations* ($3) and *Statute of the International Court of Justice* ($3).

Additional information is available from the United Nations Information Centre and documents and films can be borrowed from the Centre's Library.

Contact: United Nations Information Center, 2 UN Plaza, Room 853, New York, NY 10017; 800-253-9646; or online at http://www.un.org/

Are they regular voters?

Wondering whether Bill and Hillary Clinton voted in all the various elections? You can receive a copy of their voter registration ($0.50 each), which includes their date of birth, party affiliation, and their signature for each election. In many states voter registration cards are open records.

To find out about your state, contact your county clerk. To get a copy of Bill and Hillary's cards, contact: County Clerk's Office, 401 W. Markham St., Little Rock, AR 72201; 501-340-8330.

Fix your own credit

Credit is not a four-letter word. If you are just starting out or recovering from some debt problems, you don't need to spend a fortune for a company to repair your credit rating. You can do it yourself with some help from the Federal Trade Commission.

It has several publications which explain your rights, ways to fix your own credit, credit repair scams, and more. Publications include:

- *Choosing and Using Credit Cards*

- *Building A Better Credit Record*

- *Credit and Divorce*

- *Credit and Older Americans*

- *Building a Better Credit Record*

- *Credit Repair: Self Help May Be Best*

For your free copies contact: Public Reference, Room 130, Federal Trade Commission, Washington, DC 20580-0001; 202-326-2222; or online at http://www.ftc.gov/

A memorial to those who served

The Vietnam Veterans Memorial consists of two 200-foot black granite walls inscribed with the names of those who were killed or declared missing while serving during the Vietnam War.

A poster of the memorial is available for $2.50 plus $2.75 shipping by contacting Office of Printing and Photographic Services, American History Building, Room CB-054, MRC 644, Smithsonian Institution, Washington, DC 20560; 202-357-1933; or online at http://www.si.edu/

For your summer

Chapter 23

For your summer

Show them the one that got away

Add some zip to your weekend get-togethers with your fishing buddies or impress your teacher with a report on fish or fishing. The Audio Visual Department of the Fish and Wildlife Service has an extensive collection of both black and white pictures and color slides of fish and wildlife and there is no charge for their lending service.

Contact: Audio Visuals, Fish and Wildlife Service, 18th and C Sts., NW, Washington, DC 20240; 202-208-5611; or online at http://www.fws.gov/

Secret fishing holes revealed at last

Some of the best kept secrets are kept by Uncle Sam. There are 491 national wildlife refuges on over 91 million acres of lands and waters, which enable you to catch a glimpse of a unique wildlife heritage. The publication *National Wildlife Refuges: A Visitor's Guide* lists refuges by state, as well as the facilities available such as foot trails, auto tour routes, bicycling, canoeing, hunting, fishing, bird watching, hiking, and more.

Contact: U.S. Fish and Wildlife Service, 4401 N. Fairfax Dr., Mail Stop 130 Webb, Arlington, VA 22203; 703-358-1711; or online at http://www.refugenet.com/nwrs.htm

Boating and you

Spending a lot of time on your boat this summer? Make sure you follow all the boating safety rules, so your fun-filled summer is accident free.

For information on safety tips, the Coast Guard Hotline has a free "Boating Safety Information" packet, which includes fact sheets on safe boating, federal regulations, sources of boating education, and more. You can also request a free *Water 'N Kids* coloring book for 4-8 year olds, which explains basic concepts of water safety.

Contact: U.S. Coast Guard (OPB-2) Navigation Center, 7323 Telegraph Rd., Alexandria, VA 22310-3998; 800-368-5647; or online at http://www. uscgboating.org/

Go to the source

Boat/U.S. Equipment Catalog is a free booklet, produced under a Coast Guard grant, that describes boating services and products (many of which are free) available from more than 100 resources. You can find information on marine radios, charts, boat registration, Coast Guard requirements, and more.

Contact: BOAT/US Foundation, 880 S. Pickett St., Alexandria, VA 22304; 703-823-9550; or online at http://www.boatus.com/

Importing pleasure boats

Buying your speed boat or yacht somewhere other than in the U.S.?

The free pamphlet, *Pleasure Boats*, explains the Customs formalities involving pleasure boats to help you plan your importation and reporting requirements, overtime charges, and provides other information relating strictly to pleasure boats.

Contact: Public Information Office, U.S. Customs Service, P.O. Box 7407, Washington, DC 20044; 317-290-3149, ext. 1; or online at http://www.customs. ustreas.gov/

Updates for mariners

The free *Local Notice to Mariners* is issued weekly by each of the 10 U.S. Coast Guard districts, for small craft owners using the intracoastal waterways, other waterways and small harbors. It includes items such as chart updates, information on drawbridge operation, and warnings of a variety of events or activities.

For a subscription you should contact: Your local Coast Guard District Commander, or for referral to the correct address contact: Boating Safety Hotline, Commandant (G-NAB-5), U.S. Coast Guard Headquarters, Washington, DC 20593; 800-368-5647; or online at http://www.uscg.mil/

Stern and bow

Before you solo, take a free lesson from the U.S. Coast Guard Auxiliary which offers beginner boating lessons free of charge.

To find the location nearest you contact: U.S. Department of Transportation, U.S. Coast Guard, 2100 Second St., SW, Washington, DC 20593; 202-267-0955, 800-368-5647; or online at http://www.uscg.mil/

Man overboard

Actually, it is more common than you think. There were 458 vessels that capsized last year causing 248 deaths, and 433 vessels reporting people falling overboard with 212 deaths. Statistical information is available on a yearly basis in a free report, *Boating Statistics*.

For your copy, contact: U.S. Coast Guard (OPB-2) Navigation Center, 7323 Telegraph Rd., Alexandria, VA 22310-3998; 800-368-5647; or online at http://www.nsc.org/news/boatstat.htm

For your teacher

Chapter 24

For your teacher

Save the rainforests

We have all been told to save the rainforest, but do you want to learn more about its importance?

A free teaching guide, *Tropical Rainforests*, is available that highlights the workings of the rainforest, the adaptations of its animals and plants, their current status and future conservation. Teachers' and students' versions are available, and are designed for grades 5-12.

Contact: Smithsonian Tropical Research Institute, Office of Education, 900 Jefferson Dr., SW, MRC-435, Washington, DC 20560; 202-786-2817; or online at http://www.stri.org/

Take your class to the park

Kids will learn more at the nearest national park than they will on any rainy day indoors. Most parks have education programs and will gladly share their wonderful resources with you.

A special 28-minute video, "Parks as Classrooms", is available at your nearest park and details the many ways teachers can work with the park service and incorporate parks into their curriculum.

For information and location of parks near you contact: Office of Education and Interpretation, National Park Service Areas, U.S. Department of the Interior, P.O. Box 37127, Washington, DC 20013; 202-523-5270; or online at http://www.nps.gov/interp/parkclass.html

Your guide to outer space

Want to know what is going on in outer space? You can get a direct line to the National Aeronautics and Space Administration (NASA) through its free quarterly report, *NASA Report to Educators*. This report contains educational information, including information on technology spinoffs, new publications and resource materials, conferences, and ongoing programs and competitions.

Write your request on school letterhead and send it to the NASA Teacher Resource Center (TRC) nearest you. To find the closest TRC, call the NASA Publication Center at 202-554-4380; or online at http://www.osgc. org/nasa_trc/trc.html

Environmental hazards in your school

New York City's asbestos problem in their public schools is only the tip of the iceberg. Lead in drinking water, poor air quality, and more occur in schools across the country.

To find out about the dangers in a school and what you can do to protect your children, request a free copy of *Environmental Hazards In Your School: A Resource Handbook*, which outlines each problem and gives direction on who you need to contact to resolve the issue.

Contact: Environmental Protection Agency TSCA Assistance Service (7408), c/o Garcia Consulting, 401 M St., SW, Washington, DC 20024; 202-554-1404; or online at http://www.epa.gov/ncepihom/

Bring your paints to school

The Arts-In-Education Program is a partnership through cooperative efforts of the Arts Endowment, state arts and education agencies, local communities, and others.

The Program's overall goal is to advance the arts as part of basic education. For free information on how you can help promote the arts from kindergarten through high school, request the following free publications:

- *Understanding How the Arts Contribute to Excellent Education*

- *Arts in Schools: Perspectives from Four Nations*

- *State Arts Agency Arts in Education Profiles*

- *Schools, Communities and the Arts: A Research Compendium*

Contact: Office of Communication, Room 614, 1100 Pennsylvania Ave., NW, Washington, DC 20506; 202-682-5426; or online at http://www. nea.org

In the footsteps of T-Rex...Utah Canyon boasts fossils galore

Does the idea of a hike make your kids run the other way? What if the hike included a hunt for dinosaur bones? Mill Canyon Dinosaur Trail is a self-guided walking tour on Bureau of Land Management Lands where you will see dinosaur bones and other wonderful fossils.

For a free brochure, write: Grand Resource Center, Bureau of Land Management, 82 E. Dogwood, Moab, UT 84532; 801-259-2100; or online at http://www.blm.gov/

Ocean planet

Ocean Planet: Interdisciplinary Marine Science Activities is a 64-page teaching guide which explores topics such as ocean currents, undersea topography, the stranding of marine animals, oceans as a source of consumer goods, and water pollution. The guide contains background information, lesson plans, activity sheets, and maps.

This guide is targeted for grades 6-12. You can request your copy by contacting: Office of Education, Smithsonian Institution, Arts and Industries Building, 900 Jefferson Dr., SW, Room 1163, MRC 402, Washington, DC 20560; 202-357-2425; or online at http://educate.si.edu/lessons/currkits/ocean/main.html

Them bones, them bones

Anthropology is much more fun when you pass around real fossils instead of pictures. Bring history to life with artifacts from the Smithsonian archives.

Anthropological Materials Available From The Smithsonian Institution is a free list of educational materials, including resource packets, films, posters and more.

Contact: Anthropology Outreach and Public Information Office, National Museum of Natural History, MRC 112, Smithsonian Institution, Washington, DC 20560; 202-357-1592; or online at http://www.mnh.si.edu/

Armchair archeologists

Participate in Archeology is a free brochure which provides some basic information on archeology, and lists magazines, books, videos, and agencies and organizations through which you can receive more information.

Contact: Publications, Archeology and Ethnography Program, National Park Service, 1849 C St., NW, Washington, DC 20240; 202-343-4101; or online at http://www.nps.gov/aad/

Send your students to the moon

Rockets: A Teaching Guide for an Elementary Science Unit on Rocketry contains information on the history of rocketry, Newton's laws, and modern practical rocketry. Ten activities are included utilizing simple and inexpensive materials culminating in a model rocket launch.

For your free copy and other information available for teachers, contact the NASA Teacher Resource Center (TRC) nearest you. To find the closest TRC, contact the NASA Publication Center at 202-554-4380; or online at http://www.hq.nasa.gov/office/codef/education/index.html

Explore Mars

Exploring Mars: For Grades 5-12 gives a detailed overview of National Aeronautics and Space Administration (NASA) exploration from 1964 to 2003. It explains the major research capabilities of particular missions and expands on what further study is warranted on the red planet. Teachers are provided with activities to further engage students and basic step-by-step directions on how to explore a planet are given.

Write your request on school letterhead and send it to the NASA Teacher Resource Center (TRC) nearest you. To find the closest TRC, call the NASA Publication Center at 202-554-4380; or online at http://www.hq.nasa. gov/office/codef/education/index.html

Learn to work, work to learn

Vocational education is a hot topic for students and schools. The National Center for Research in Vocational Education (NCRVE), supported by the U.S. Department of Education, is the nation's largest center for research and development in work-related education. NCRVE's mission is to strengthen education to prepare all individuals for lasting and rewarding employment and lifelong learning.

NCRVE has put together a number of informative documents on vocational education, including:

- *Learning How to Learn at Work: Lessons From Three High School Programs*

- *Getting to Work: A Guide for Better Schools*

- *Integrating Academic and Industrial Skill Standards*

- *Meeting Teachers' Professional Development Needs for School to Work Transition*

For more information, contact: NCRVE, University of California, Berkeley, 2030 Addison St., Suite 500, Berkeley, CA 94720-1674; 800-762-4093; or online at http://ncrve.berkeley.edu/

Everything old is new again

Have you ever wondered how the earliest inhabitants of North America lived? Interested in what goes on at an archeological dig? Heritage Education program is a very hands-on learning experience aimed at students K-12 with projects and traveling exhibitions.

For a free brochure and other information, contact: The Imagination Team, Bureau of Land Management, Anasazi Heritage Center, 27501 Hwy 184, P.O. Box 758, Dolores, CO 81323; 970-882-4811; or online at http://www.co.blm.gov/ahc/hmepge.htm

Shaking in their seats

Earthquakes and volcanoes are like dinosaurs: timeless and totally awesome. Use this to your advantage when teaching geology.

The Geologic Inquiries Group has a free publication, *Educational Resources Available From The U.S. Geological Survey*, which describes teacher packets, booklets, and other resources available to teachers.

Please send your request on school letterhead to: U.S. Geological Survey, Reston Earth Science Information Center, 507 National Center, Reston, VA 20192; 800-USA-MAPS; or online at http://www.usgs.gov/

Art of the U.S.

All the great artists are not from Europe. The U.S. has its fair share.

The National Museum of American Art focuses on these artists and their work and has assembled a collection of brochures, teaching guides, and exhibition catalogues.

• *African-American Art: 19th and 20th Century Selections*—each page has an illustration and background text on a work.

• *National Museum of American Art and its Renwick Gallery*— bimonthly brochure with brief descriptions and images from collection.

Contact: National Museum of American Art, Office of Educational Programs, MRC 210, Smithsonian Institution, Washington, DC 20560; 202-357-2247; or online at http://www.nmaa.si.edu/

Cloudy with a chance of eagles

Want a tailor-made package of materials to hand out to teach students about the weather? The National Oceanic and Atmospheric Administration will pull one together—just specify grade and subject. Topics covered include the weather, oceans, whales, marine mammals, nautical charts, fisheries, and more.

Write: U.S. Department of Commerce/NOAA, PA/Correspondence Unit, 1305 East-West Highway, Silver Springs, MD 20910; 301-713-1208; or online at http://www.noaa.gov/public_affairs/teachers.html

Speak out

Teaching about the Civil Rights movement? *Protest and Patriotism: A History of Dissent and Reform* is a teaching guide ($5) containing curriculum enrichment materials examining American protest movements.

It focuses on populism, civil rights, and environmentalism. The guide provides background essays, discussion questions, teaching suggestions, and a timeline. This is designed for grades 7-12.

For your copy contact: Office of Education, Smithsonian Institution, Arts & Industries Building, 900 Jefferson Dr., SW, Room 1163 MRC 402, Washington, DC 20560; 202-357-2425; or online at http://educate.si.edu/

You and your wildlife

Many animals are more abundant in the U.S. now than in the past 100 years.

In Celebration of America's Wildlife: Teacher's Guide to Learning is a video and curriculum guide, which provides information about the Federal Aid in Wildlife Restoration Act, and lists activities and discussions related to the major concepts of the video.

Contact: U.S. Fish and Wildlife Service, 1849 C St., NW, Room 3444, Washington, DC 20240; 304-876-7203; or online at http://www.fws.gov/~bennishk/pubs.html

Where the heck Is Timbuktu?

Have students identify places with the funniest names, then find out more about the lay of the land. With a request on school letterhead, the Earth Science Center will put together special packages on geography for teachers.

Contact: U.S. Geological Survey, Reston Earth Science Information Center, 507 National Center, Reston, VA 20192; 800-USA-MAPS; or online at http://www.usgs.gov/

Bring a cast-iron umbrella

Acid Rain: A Student's First Sourcebook is a great way to teach kids about the environment and what needs to be done to protect it. Designed for grades 4-8 and their teachers, the sourcebook describes the effects of acid rain, solutions, experiments, and activities.

This office also has U.S. Environmental Protection Agency (EPA) Journal articles on acid rain, background information, and updates on EPA's activities.

Contact: Acid Rain Division (6204J), Environmental Protection Agency, 401 M St., SW, Washington, DC 20460; 202-564-9620; or online at http://www.epa.gov/acidrain/student/student2.html

The noble path

The Noble Path ($4.50) is a booklet which provides an introduction to Buddhism and Buddhist art, with background information for teachers, activities for students, and a list of related videos and films.

Contact: Arthur M. Sackler Gallery, Education Department, MRC 707, Smithsonian Institution, Washington, DC 20560; 202-357-4880; or online at http://www.si.edu/organiza/museums/freer/html/curricul.htm

Scientific Americans

Fire up the Bunsen burners and full speed ahead. Science teachers can send off for course materials, curriculum guides, and more on a wide range of science projects, courtesy of the National Science Resources Center (NSRC).

A free information packet is available by contacting the Outreach Department, Room 1201, National Science Resources Center, 900 Jefferson Dr., SW, Washington, DC 20560; 202-287-2064; or online at http://www.si.edu/nsrc/nsrc.html

Build a better light bulb

Can creativity be taught? Project XL is an outreach program designed to do just that by encouraging the inventive thinking process through the creation of unique inventions or innovations. They have developed an educator's resource guide, video, and a special curriculum.

Request your free copy of the *Inventive Thinking Project*. Contact: Office of Public Affairs, Patent and Trademark Office, U.S. Department of Commerce, 2121 Crystal Dr., Suite 0100, Crystal Park II, Washington DC 22202; 703-305-8341; or online at http://www.uspto.gov/

Make African art come alive

Whether for art history or to study the various cultures in Africa, take advantage of your students' love of videos and use videos and slide kits available from the National Museum of African Art.

- "The Hands of the Potter" is a video demonstrating the magic of a Sundi potter as she forms moist clay to produce perfect pots.

- "African Art in the Collection" is a group of forty slides and explanatory text introducing significant works from the museum's permanent collection.

- "Masters of Brass: Lost-Wax Casting in Ghana" demonstrates the ancient technique among the Akan and Frafra peoples of Ghana in which a wax model is used to create a mold for casting a metal object.

For free loan information and to find out about the many other programs available contact: National Museum of African Art, Department of Education, MRC 708, 950 Independence Ave., SW, Smithsonian Institution, Washington, DC 20560; 202-357-4600; or online at http://www.si.edu/organiza/museums/africart/

Smokey the Bear posters

To make children aware of the campaign to fight forest fires, the Forest Service makes a variety of free materials available to children, including posters, signs, patches, bookmarks, bumper stickers, and comic books.

Contact your local forest service division, or to find a coordinator in your area who has a list of materials available, contact: Smokey Bear Headquarters,

U.S. Forest Service, 14th and Independence Aves., NW, Washington, DC 20250; 202-205-1510; or online at http://www.smokeybear.com/

The original Jurassic playground

By now, most of America has seen the movie "Jurassic Park", but the real Jurassic story can be found on Bureau of Land Management lands in the West.

One of the largest areas is the Cleveland-Lloyd Dinosaur Quarry, which has yielded nearly 10,000 bones representing at least 14 species of animals from the Jurassic Period.

For a copy of a free brochure describing the quarry titled, *Al the Allosaurus*, write: Price River Resource Area Office, Bureau of Land Management, 125 South 6 West, Price, UT 84501; 801-636-3600; or online at http://www.utah.com/destin/coloradop/cppublic/blmcl.htm

Indian ancestry

Make the American Indians section come alive in your classroom. The Anthropology Outreach Office has a free teaching packet titled *North American Indians* for grades 1-12, which includes bibliographies, leaflets, lists of teaching materials available from the Smithsonian, photographs, suggestions for classroom activities, and even information on Native American pen-pals.

For your copy, contact: Anthropology Outreach and Public Information Office, National Museum of Natural History, Room 363, MRC 112, Smithsonian Institution, Washington, DC 20560; 202-357-1592; or online at http://www.nmnh.si.edu/

Powwow with the experts

Get a glimpse of the rich cultural heritage of our Native American history. Many tribes continue to celebrate customs that were old before Columbus reached shore.

The Bureau of Indian Affairs has a free publication, *American Indians and Alaska Natives*, which provides a brief overview, as well as providing a bibliography and other resources. This office can also provide you with other information on Indians including statistics, locations of reservations, and more.

Contact: Public Inquiries, Bureau of Indian Affairs, 1849 C St., NW, Washington, DC 20240; 202-208-3338; or online at http://128.174.5.51/denix/public/native/outreach/american/indian.html

Drug abuse teaching aids

The Office of Educational Research and Improvement of the U.S. Department of Education has developed several publications dealing with substance abuse curriculum.

• *Learning to Live Drug Free: A Curriculum Model for Prevention* provides a framework for classroom-based prevention efforts in kindergarten through grade 12. The model includes lessons, activities, background for teachers and suggestions for involving parents and the community in drug prevention.

• *Toward a Drug-Free Generation: A Nation's Responsibility.*

• *Success Stories from Drug-Free Schools.*

• *Parents Getting a Head Start Against Drugs.*

• *Drug Abuse Prevention for At-Risk Groups.*

Contact: National Clearinghouse for Alcohol and Drug Information, P.O. Box 2345, Rockville, MD 20847; 800-729-6686; or online at http://www.health.org

Wild and woolly neighborhoods

You don't have to hire a guide and rent tents to experience the wonders of a wildlife refuge. There's probably one tucked right around the corner from school. Snakes, turtles, even an injured owl will make your students sit up and take notice.

Many of the National Wildlife Refuges have established education programs where refuge managers may come to your class with animals in hand or your class may take a trip to the refuge. This varies from place to place, but give the wildlife refuge near you a call to see what services they offer.

For a publication titled *Refuge Managers List* contact: U.S. Fish and Wildlife Service, U.S. Department of the Interior, 4040 N. Fairfax Dr., Arlington, VA 22203; 800-344-WILD; or online at http://refuges.fws.gov/

Help students clean up

Kids intuitively grasp recycling and the need to keep the earth green and clean, so what's with their own rooms?

Let's Reduce and Recycle: Curriculum for Solid Waste Awareness provides lesson plans for grades K-12, and includes activities, skits, bibliographies, and other resources.

School Recycling Programs: A Handbook for Educators describes a number of school recycling programs along with step-by-step instructions on how to start one in your school.

For these free publications contact: RCRA /Superfund Hotline, Office of Solid Waste, U.S. Environmental Protection Agency, 401 M St., SW, Washington, DC 20460; 800-424-9346 (Superfund hotline), 800-490-9198 (publications).

The idea factory

Art to Zoo is a free quarterly publication of the Office of Elementary and Secondary Education and provides background information, lesson plans, classroom activities, and resource lists for teachers in science, social studies, and art.

Each issue focuses on a different topic, and is designed for grades 3-8.

For your free subscription contact: Office of Elementary and Secondary Education, Smithsonian Institution, Arts and Industries Building, Room 1163 MRC 402, Washington, DC 20560; 202-357-2425.

Current and select back issues are available online at http://educate.si.edu/lessons/art-to-zoo/azindex.html

River and water films

The Bureau of Reclamation provides water for farms, towns, and industries, and is responsible for the generation of hydroelectric power, river regulation and flood control, outdoor recreation opportunities, and the enhancement and protection of fish and wildlife habitats.

There are films available for free loan on a variety of the Bureau's projects. Some of the titles include:

- "California Flooding"

- "How Water Won the West"

- "Rio Grande—Ribbon of Life"

- "To Build A Dream—The Story of Hoover Dam"

- "Take Pride in America"

- "Hydropower—A 20th Century Force"

- "A New Horizon"

- "Columbia, A Fountain of Life"

- "Challenge at Glen Canyon".

These films are most often requested by elementary and junior high school teachers, or by people who have visited the dams while on vacation and would like to learn more about them. Contact the Bureau for more information regarding these videos.

Contact: Reclamation Service Center Library, P.O. Box 25007, Building 67, Denver Federal Center, Denver, CO 80225-0007; 303-445-2072.

Art assistance

The National Gallery of Art has assembled teaching packets, available for free loan, covering specific artists or time periods. These packets usually contain a booklet, slides and study prints. A complete listing is included in the Extension Programs catalogue.

Some the packets available are:

• *Matisse in Morocco*

• *Art of the American Indian Frontier*

• *The Inquiring Eye: European Renaissance Art*

• *The American Vision*

• *French Impressionism and Post-Impressionism*

Contact: Department of Education Resources, Education Division, National Gallery of Art, 4th St. and Constitution Ave., NW, Washington, DC 20565; 202-842-6263; or online at http://www.nga.gov/resources/resource.htm

The mummy walks at midnight

Kids are fascinated by strange things. The Anthropology Outreach Office has three free leaflets available dealing with Egypt long ago.

Egyptian Mummies describes the art of mummification. *Egyptian Pyramids* describes the various types of pyramids. *Ancient Egypt* lists books and articles appropriate for adults and younger readers. These leaflets include bibliographies and are applicable for grades K-12.

Contact: Anthropology Outreach and Public Information Office, National Museum of Natural History, Room 363, MRC 112, Smithsonian Institution, Washington, DC 20560; 202-357-1592; or online at http://www.nmnh.si.edu/

Your travel journal

Get your students to pretend to be reporters on the scene. *Collecting Their Thoughts: Using Museums as Sources for Student Writing* ($5) is a teaching guide, containing curriculum enrichment materials suggesting ways for teachers to use museums and primary sources to teach writing. The Guide provides background essays, lesson plans, activities, handouts, and samples of student writing.

Contact: Office of Elementary and Secondary Education, Smithsonian Institution, Arts and Industries Building, Room 1163 MRC 402, Washington, DC 20560; 202-357-2425; or online at http://educate.si.edu/

Science horizons

Physics made easy? *Science Horizons* disseminates information about education projects underway at the Science Education Department of the Harvard-Smithsonian Center for Astrophysics, including summer workshops for teachers, the development of software for the simulation of modern physics, and highly sensitive image-processing equipment for classroom use. It is free and designed for grades 1-12.

Contact: Harvard-Smithsonian Center for Astrophysics, Science Education Department, MS-71, 60 Garden St., Cambridge, MA 01238; 617-495-9798; or online at http://cfa-www.harvard.edu/

Teaching science close to home

Intrigued by the past? Teachers can show students the importance of past cultures and archaeology with *The Intriguing Past: Fundamentals of Archeology* ($2). This teacher's guide is aimed at grades 4-7, and includes lesson plans and activity sheets.

Contact: The Imagination Team, Bureau of Land Management, Anasazi Heritage Center, 27501 Hwy 184, P.O. Box 758, Dolores, CO 81323; 970-882-4811; or online at http://www.co.blm.gov/ahc/hmepge.htm

Turn the tide

Two-thirds of our planet is covered by oceans which are homes for thousands of species of plants and animals. Unfortunately ocean trash and other wastes are becoming a significant problem.

Turning the Tide on Trash: Learning Guide on Marine Debris ($27) is designed to increase students' awareness of the impacts of marine debris and to teach them about pollution prevention techniques. The activities also inspire an appreciation of the ocean and a commitment to the preservation of its water quality and beauty.

For your copy, contact: National Technical Information Service, 5285 Port Royal Rd., Springfield, VA 22161; 703-487-4650, 800-553-NTIS; or online at http://www.ntis.gov/. You can also look at selected portions of the guide on the web at http://www.epa.gov/owow/ocpd/marine/contents.html

Following in Godzilla's footsteps

The Smithsonian is the granddaddy of museums, but like T-Rex, its size can be a bit of a problem. Fortunately there's a special booklet to help teachers get their bearings when navigating through the Smithsonian's musty closets. The publication, *Smithsonian Resource Guide For Teachers* ($5), lists workshops, courses, publications and newsletters for teachers across the country, most of which are free.

Contact: Office of Elementary and Secondary Education, Smithsonian Institution, Arts & Industries Building, Room 1163 MRC 402, Washington, DC 20560; 202-357-2425; or online at http://educate.si.edu/resource/

Hands-on science

Resources for Teaching Elementary School Science is a 312-page guide to hands-on science teaching materials from the United States and abroad for elementary school teachers and administrators.

It includes materials in life science, health and human biology, earth science, physical science, and multidisciplinary and applied science. Each entry provides descriptions of curriculum materials, suggestions for supplementary resources and sources of information and assistance, and details relating to source, grade levels, orders, and cost.

The book costs $17.95 plus $4 shipping and handling; there is a discount for multiple copies. The cost is $14.36 if you order online.

Contact: National Academy Press, 2101 Constitution Ave., NW, Box 285, Washington, DC 20055; 202-334-3313, 800-624-6242; or online at http://www.nap.edu/bookstore

One with nature

Many Native American tribes believe we should live in harmony with nature. Here's a great coloring book to teach the concept to kids, courtesy of the Flathead Indian Reservation.

Living In Harmony coloring book ($1.35) is distributed by National Association of Conservation Districts, 408 East Main, P.O. Box 855, League City, TX 77574; 800-825-5547; or online at http://www.nacdnet.org/

Draw me a map

The Power of Maps is a free teaching guide with suggestions on integrating the study of maps into school curricula based on the exhibition "The Power of Maps" at Cooper Hewitt. It includes suggestions for classroom activities, discussion questions, and a resource list.

Contact: Cooper-Hewitt National Museum of Design, Education Department, Smithsonian Institution, 2 East 91st St., New York, NY 10128; 212-849-8385; or online at http://www.si.edu/ndm/

Social Studies simplified

Elementary and secondary school teachers, policymakers, even parents concerned about education in the social studies are likely to be interested in the activities and publications of the ERIC Clearinghouse on Social Studies, which monitors trends and issues about the teaching and learning of history, geography, civics, economics, and other subjects.

A free newsletter, *Keeping Up*, describes the latest information in the field. The Clearinghouse also produces several digests, which are synopses of current literature on a topic of interest to social studies educators. The price of a digest is $1, and some of the titles include:

• *Computers and Art Education*

• *Teaching About Democratic Constitutionalism*

• *Teaching About Africa*

• *We The People: The Citizen and the Constitution*

• *Teaching About Vietnam and the Vietnam War*

For a complete listing of publications contact: ERIC Clearinghouse For Social Studies, Indiana University, Social Studies Development Center, 2805 East 10th St., Suite 120, Bloomington, IN 47408; 812-855-3838; 800-266-3815; or online at http://www.indiana.edu/~ssdc/eric_chess.htm

Every day should be Earth Day

"Earth Day Teacher's Kit" is a free packet available from the U.S. Environmental Protection Agency, and provides a wonderful overview of environmental science education for all grade levels. Each section lists activities, materials needed, discussion questions, vocabulary, and more. You can learn how to make a cloud, how substances are measured in water, and how rivers are formed.

For your free copy contact: National Center for Environmental Publications and Information, P.O. Box 42419, Cincinnati, OH 45242-2419; 800-490-9198; or online at http://www.epa.gov/ncepihom/

Free science lab equipment

Is the equipment in your college's laboratories broken, out-dated, or just worn out? The U.S. Department of Energy (DOE) will send your school energy-related lab equipment that they no longer need for free with you paying shipping and handling. The following publications cover the program and the equipment available: *Energy-Related Laboratory Equipment Catalog,* and *Instruction and Information On Used Energy-Related Equipment Grants for Educational Institutions of Higher Learning* ($12.50).

Contact: Postsecondary Programs Division, Office of University and Science Education, Office of Energy Research, DOE, ET-31, Washington, DC 20585; 202-586-8947; or online at http://www.petc.doe.gov/business/prop.html

Sitting Bull

For a great visual aid to your unit on Native Americans, you can get a wonderful poster of Sitting Bull, who led the Sioux Indians in the Battle of Little Big Horn. The 21x28" poster in sepia tone is available for $3.

Contact: Office of Printing and Photographic Services, American History Building, Room CB-054, MRC 644, Smithsonian Institution, Washington, DC 20560; 202-357-1933; or online at http://photo2.si.edu/index.html

Getting smart, smarter, smartest

Want to know about the number of people over 50 returning to college, or how kids do in school if they go to preschool?

The National Education Bulletin Board from the Office of Educational Research and Development extends its free electronic bulletin board services to persons employed in the field of education. Services range from the Library of Congress access to the National Education Supercomputer (NES).

For access, call 800-447-6377, and select http://nebbs.llnl.gov (Note: this address opens a "telnet" connection. At the "login" prompt, type "nebbs").

Outer space is just a phone call away

Teachers who wish to incorporate space in their education programs can find a galaxy full of information from National Aeronautics and Space Administration (NASA) Spacelink.

Educational programs include Aerospace Education Services Project, Urban Community Enrichment Program, Summer High School Apprenticeship Research Program, Teacher Workshops, Educators mailing list, tele-lectures, Teacher Resource Centers, and more.

Access is available on the Internet. Call 202-358-1110 and select http://spacelink.nasa.gov/index.html

Separation of church and state?

To give equal time to all sides, many schools are teaching creationism. The Anthropology Outreach Office has put together a free bibliography on "Creationism/Evolution" for grades 1-12, which covers issues surrounding the creationism/evolution debate, and education for teachers and administrators from all disciplines.

For your copy, contact: Anthropology Outreach and Public Information Office, National Museum of Natural History, Room 363, MRC 112, Smithsonian Institution, Washington, DC 20560; 202-357-1592; or online at http://www.nmnh.si.edu/anthro/outreach/

Make history come alive

Lift events and people off the pages of textbooks and help students connect history to their own lives.

Teaching With Historic Places (TWHP) is a program created by the National Park Service and the National Trust for Historic Preservation and is administered by the National Register. TWHP uses properties listed in the National Register of Historic Places to enliven the teaching of history, social studies, geography, civics, and other subjects. The program has created ready to use lesson plans, multifaceted education kits, and professional development materials and workshops.

For more information or a free brochure on TWHP, contact: Teaching With Historic Places, National Register of Historic Places, National Park Service, P.O. Box 37127, Suite 250, Washington, DC 20013-7127; 202-343-9536; or online at http://www.nps.gov/crweb1/nr/twhp/home.html

Adventures in the past

Help your students learn about archaeology and caring for the environment in an interesting and new way.

The Bureau of Land Management (BLM) is caretaker of an estimated 5 million historic and archaeological properties on almost 300 million acres of land. *BLM's Adventures in the Past* program is designed to capture the attention of your students and create excitement in the study of history and archaeology. There are many different segments of this program, including:

• *Project Archaeology*—classroom activities in archaeology to enrich classroom teaching.

• *Set in Stone*—posters, lessons, and teacher guides on the study of fossils.

- *Mystery of the Mesa*—a science detective story with adventures for teachers and students.

- *Steel Rails and Iron Horses*—the story of the railroads and the march across the west.

To learn more about what is available, contact your nearest BLM office, or the Environmental Education and Volunteers Team, Bureau of Land Management, 1275 LS, 1849 C St., NW, Washington, DC 20240; 202-452-5078; or online at http://www.blm.gov/education/teacher.html

Grab their attention!

How can you get your student's attention? With audio-visual educational materials from NTIS' National Audiovisual Center.

Bring your lessons to life with exciting and informative videos from the National Audiovisual Center's collection. From life and death issues such as drugs and safety awareness to understanding the responsibilities of citizenship; from environmental and minority issues to history from pre-Columbian times to the present, these videotapes will capture your students' attention and help them learn.

These programs are prepared by experts in the field under the sponsorship of federal agencies such as the Department of Education, Smithsonian Institution, National Aeronautics and Space Administration, Department of Health and Human Services, Environmental Protection Agency, and National Park Service. Many of the programs have won prestigious awards.

For more information, and a free catalog of resources, contact: National Audiovisual Center, National Technical Information Service, Technology

Administration, U.S. Department of Commerce, Springfield, VA 22161; 703-487-4349; or online at http://www.ntis.gov/nac/nac.htm

Keeping your head in the stars and your feet in math and science

There's a free information clearinghouse to help teachers and students perform well in math and science.

To improve access to mathematics and science resources available to teachers, students, parents, and others, the clearinghouse collects and creates the most up-to-date and comprehensive listing of mathematics and science curriculum materials in the nation. A list or catalog is available on several mediums.

You can also get a free (while supplies last) copy of *Guidebook to Excellence*, which is a directory by region of federal resources for math and science education improvement.

Contact: Eisenhower National Clearinghouse for Mathematics and Science Education, The Ohio State University, 1929 Kenny Rd., Columbus, OH 43210-1079; 614-292-7784, 800-276-0462; or online at http://www.enc.org/

How do you keep up?

Most teachers barely have the time to prepare for their own classes, much less keep current on new publications in their field. The National Library of Education's Reference and Information Services Division can help.

The Division provides a current literature awareness service (CLAS) to Department of Education staff. CLAS is subject-oriented computer printouts providing abstracts, bibliographic information and/or citations of literature announced each week or month from selected databases. The public can request copies of any of these reports on a wide range of educational topics.

For more information, contact: U.S. Department of Education, OERI, National Library of Education, 555 New Jersey Ave., NW, Room 101, Washington, DC 20208-5721; 202-219-1692; or online at http://www.ed.gov/nle/fact6.html

History 101

The National Register of Historic Places is this nation's official list of cultural resources worthy of preservation. These places are maintained by the National Park Service and include sites, buildings, structures, archaeology, architecture, engineering, and culture. Several publications are available free of charge, including:

- *National Register of Historic Places Brochure*

- *National Register of Historic Places Information Sheet*

- *Cultural Diversity and Historic Preservation*

- *Using the National Register of Historic Places*

Write: National Register of Historic Places, National Park Service, 1849 C St., NW, Washington, DC 20240; or online at http://www.cr.nps.gov/nr/nrhome.html

English as a second language and bilingual education

Today's classroom doesn't look quite the same as it did 20 years ago. Teachers find more students are barely able to speak English. The National Clearinghouse for Bilingual Education (NCBE) can help teachers and families by providing information such as curriculum materials, models, and research findings on educating those with limited English.

NCBE's web site (http://www.ncbe.gwu.edu) has a wealth of free resources that can be used for classroom instruction, student assessment, teacher training, program development, research, and grant applications. The "Online Library" contains hundreds of full-length articles, reports, guides, and other documents on topics such as school reform and student diversity, family literacy, parent involvement, and effective schooling for language minority students.

NCBE also offers a free reference and referral service to help educators and parents locate additional resources; and a weekly e-mail news bulletin, *Newsline*, which provides subscribers with the latest developments relating to the education of linguistically and culturally diverse students.

For more information about NCBE's services, or to request a newsletter or publication catalog, contact: National Clearinghouse for Bilingual Education, 1118 22nd St., NW, Washington, DC 20037; 202-467-0867, Fax: 800-531-9347; E-mail: askncbe@ncbe.gwu.edu; or online at http://www. ncbe.gwu.edu

African-American art

If you are teaching your students about African-Americans, don't forget to include information about their art.

African-American Art: 20th Century Selections is a 13 page brochure which examines the work of 12 African-American artists who triumphed over discrimination and limited opportunities for training, patronage, and exhibitions to make significant contributions to America's cultural heritage. This is designed for grades 5-12.

For your copy contact: Office of Educational Programs, National Museum of American Art, MRC 210, Smithsonian Institution, Washington, DC 20560; 202-357-3095; or online at http://www.nmaa.si.edu/

For your travels

25

Chapter 25

For your travels

Know before you go

Can you bring back a kangaroo coat you purchased in Australia? What do you have to declare? Can you mail packages home from abroad and not declare the items? All these are important questions to ask before you let your charge cards loose in a foreign country.

The Customs Service has several interesting free pamphlets to get you headed in the right direction. *Know Before You Go* explains what you can and cannot bring into the country and explains what you must declare. *International Mail Imports* explains the rules regarding mailing packages from abroad.

For either of these publications write: U.S. Customs Service, P.O. Box 7407, Washington, DC 20044; 202-927-2095; or online at http://www.customs.ustreas.gov/

Right-on write-offs

There's still time to take advantage of leftover tax laws that favor the well-heeled. The Internal Revenue Service (IRS) has changed some of the rules regarding business deductions, but there are still ways you can write off parts of your summer vacation as a business expense. Anyone can do it, even if you're just an employee.

To find out how, ask for a free copy of *Publication 463, Travel, Entertainment, Gift and Car Expenses,* by contacting the IRS at 800-829-3676, or online at http://www.irs.gov/

Far shores, far out

Want to study art in Italy? How about orangutans in Sumatra?

The Youth Programs Division of the U.S. Information Agency sponsors a bunch of exchange programs for daring young rebels. Awards aren't made to individuals, but to the International Education Travel and Exchange Programs which in turn sponsor youth between the ages of 15 and 30.

A free listing of these programs titled *Advisory List of International Educational Travel and Exchange Programs* can be obtained from: Youth Programs Division, United States Information Agency, 301 4th St., SW, Room 314, Washington, DC 20547; 202-619-6299; or online at http://www.usia.gov/

Where to go

Deciding your vacation itinerary? *The Recreation Guide to BLM Public Lands* features a map outlining all of the public lands used as recreational areas. Designations on the map include campgrounds, visitors centers, national wild and scenic rivers, national wilderness areas, and national historic and scenic trails. Also included are the states that contain public lands, and state and district offices to contact for additional information.

Contact: Office of Public Affairs, Bureau of Land Management, U.S. Department of the Interior, 18th and C Sts., NW, Washington, DC 20240; 202-208-3171; or online at http://www.blm.gov

Fly right

Which airline has the best ontime rate? Who loses the least amount of luggage? Which airport keeps on schedule the best? On which airline are you least likely to get bumped?

All of the answers to these questions and more are available from *The Air Travel Consumer Report*, a monthly report issued by the Office of Consumer Affairs at the U.S. Department of Transportation.

For your free copy contact: Aviation Consumer Protection Division, U.S. Department of Transportation, 400 7th St., SW, Washington, DC 20590; 202-366-9342; or online at http://www.dot.gov/ost/ogc/subject/consumer/aviation/data/atcr/index.htm

Take the train

Fascinated by train travel? AMTRAK has a deal for you. They publish a travel planner which provides travel tips and services, as well as a listing of AMTRAK's vacation packages.

For your free copy contact: AMTRAK, 60 Massachusetts Ave., NE, Washington, DC 20002; 800-USA-RAIL; or online at http://www.amtrak.com/

Why are you taking my...?

Avoid the embarrassment in Customs when your suitcase is emptied and confiscated. Know what you can and cannot bring back to the U.S. before you go.

- *Travelers Alert!* alerts travelers to the requirement to declare all fruits, vegetables, meat, plants, and more.

- *Travelers' Tips* lists what food, plant, and animal products can and cannot be brought into the U.S. from foreign countries.

- *Why Are You Taking My...?* is for inspectors to give to travelers explaining why items were confiscated.

Contact: Animal and Plant Health Inspection Service, U.S. Department of Agriculture, 4700 River Rd., Unit 1A, Riverdale, MD 20737; 301-734-4821; or online at http://www.aphis.usda.gov/

Travel scams

Have you ever been tempted to buy one of those bargain-priced travel packages sold over the telephone? Be careful. Your dream vacation may turn into a misadventure if you fall victim to one of the many travel scams being sold over the phone which are defrauding consumers out of millions of dollars each month.

If you feel you are a victim of just such a scam, or you want information on how to avoid them, request the free pamphlet, *Telemarketing Travel Fraud*.

Contact: Federal Trade Commission, Marketing Practices, 6th and Pennsylvania Ave., NW, Washington, DC 20580; 202-326-3128; or online at http://www.ftc.gov/

Camp USA

The national forests are truly America's great outdoors; 155 stretch from Alaska to Puerto Rico and offer outstanding opportunities for outdoor recreation.

Wherever you are, you're probably no more than a day's drive from a national forest, where you can hike, fish, camp, ski, or just sit back and enjoy the forest surroundings.

A Guide To Your National Forests is a free publication which lists regional Forest Service offices, as well as addresses and phone numbers for each national forest. Request your free guide today.

Contact: Forest Service, U.S. Department of Agriculture, 201 14th St., SW, Washington, DC 20250; 202-205-0957; or online at http://www.fs.fed.us/

Call Mother Nature

Tired of the rat race and need some time to contemplate the meaning of life? Head to the woods for some relaxation.

To find out more about the National Parks, such as facilities, activities, and accommodations, request a free "National Parks System Map and Guide" packet. This includes a listing of the most frequently visited parks, regional park service offices, reservation information, and more.

Contact: Office of Public Inquiries, National Park Service, U.S. Department of the Interior, P.O. Box 37127, Washington, DC 20013-7127; 202-208-4747; or online at http://www.nps.gov/

Travel on Uncle Sam's expense account

Are you an expert on a particular topic? Are you an artist? The U.S. Speakers Program will pay experts to travel abroad and participate in seminars, colloquia or symposia. Subjects treated by the program include economics, international political relations, U.S. social and political processes, arts and humanities, and science and technology.

To see if you qualify, contact: U.S. Speakers, Office of Program Coordination and Development, U.S. Information Agency, 301 4th St., SW, Room 550, Washington, DC 20547; 202-619-4764; or online at http://www.usia.gov/

George Washington never slept here

The Advisory Council on Historic Places reviews federal policies and procedures regarding preservation and enhancement of historic properties. They also maintain a free list of State Historic Preservation Officers, who can tell you about historic and archeological sites in their states, as well as direct you to the appropriate information sources.

Contact: Advisory Council on Historic Preservation, 1100 Pennsylvania Ave., NW, Suite 809, Washington, DC 20004; 202-606-8503; or online at http://achp.gov

Before you set to sea...

Better check the weather. The Office of Aeronautical Charting and Cartography (AC&C) provides free information for mariners, marine advisories, global positioning, and chart correction for ocean-going ships. A weekly newsletter is published with charts and graphics, but electronic news is available immediately.

For customer service information, contact: AC&C at 301-436-6990; or online at http://.acc.nos.noaa.gov/

Plague in Patagonia?

When travelling to the far reaches of the earth, or perhaps to the country next door, how can you be sure there isn't a raging epidemic that would spoil your plans?

The Center for Disease Control (CDC) has an extensive international travel web site where you can search by country or disease, obtain vaccination recommendations, examine food and water suggestions, and much more.

Call the CDC at 404-332-4559, or take a look at the web site at http://www.cdc.gov/travel/travel.html

3-2-1-Lift off!

Want to see a shuttle lift off from the Kennedy Space Center, or just learn more about the Center? The John F. Kennedy Space Center will provide an information packet for those who want to learn more about the Space Center's accomplishments and function. Great for those wanting to learn more about space!

Contact: John F. Kennedy Space Center, NASA BOC-155, Kennedy Space Center, FL 32899; 407-867-4050; or online at http://www.ksc.nasa.gov/

Do some research

Going to a country where you've never been before? *Background Notes on the Countries of the World* is a series of short, factual pamphlets with information on the country's land, people, history, government, political conditions, economy, foreign relations, and U.S. foreign policy. Each pamphlet also includes a factual profile, brief travel notes, a country map, and a reading list.

Most *Background Notes* are now available online at http://www.state.gov/www/background_notes/index.html. For more information, contact: Public Affairs Bureau, U.S. Department of State, Room 4827A, 2201 C St., NW, Washington, DC 20520; 202-647-2518.

An annual subscription to the entire *Background Note* series can be purchased through the U.S. Government Printing Office. Contact: Superintendent of Documents, U.S. Government Printing Office, Washington, DC 20402; 202-512-1800.

Row, row, row your boat

Don't get lost up-creek without a paddle. The Army Corps of Engineers can teach you the proper way to handle a canoe or tie a line. They have a series of ten free brochures describing what recreation areas and services are available all over the country.

Contact: ACE Publications Depot, 2803 52nd Ave., Hyattsville, MD 20781; 301-394-0081; or online at http://www.usace.army.mil/

Pearls and perfume, shavers and skis—tax free?

The Generalized System of Preferences is an agreement used by many developed countries to help developing nations improve their financial or economic condition through exports. In effect, it provides for the duty-free importation of a wide range of products that would otherwise be subject to customs duty if imported from non-GSP-status countries.

Approximately 4,284 items have been designed as eligible for duty-free treatment from selected countries. You can obtain the publication *GSP and the Traveler* from the Customs Service which tells more about this program, and even has a list of popular tourist items that in general have been accorded GSP status.

For more information, contact: U.S. Customs Service, U.S. Department of the Treasury, 1301 Constitution Ave., NW, Washington, DC 20229; 317-290-3149; or online at http://www.customs.ustreas.gov/

Not just a trip, but an adventure

Planning a trip to Florida and want to know about the tourist attractions? You can call or write the senator of the state you plan to visit to get information on tourist attractions. There is also information available from the Department of Tourism located in each state capitol.

Contact: Senator of your choice, The Capitol, Washington, DC 20510; 202-224-3121; or online at http://www.senate.gov/

Be your own tour guide

Stopping at all the historic places on your summer road trip?

The Office of Public Affairs can provide you with a list of publications available from the National Park Service.

They publish the *National Park Handbooks*, which are compact introductions to the great natural and historic places administered by the Park Service.

Each is intended to be informative reading and a useful guide before, during, and after a park visit. Some of the titles include:

- *Antietam National Battlefield* ($3.50)

- *Craters of the Moon National Monument* ($2.25)

- *Gettysburg National Military Park* ($2.50)

- *John Brown's Raid* ($4.25)

- *Wright Brothers National Memorial* ($2.75)

To get a free catalogue contact: The Harpers Ferry Historical Association, P.O. Box 197, Harpers Ferry, WV 25425; 304-535-6881.

For your worries

Chapter 26
For your worries

The bomb's in the mail

The likelihood of you ever receiving a bomb in the mail is extremely remote, but in fact within the past five years, over 70 such incidents have occurred.

For help in recognizing such threats request a free publication titled *Bombs By Mail* (Notice 71) from: Congressional And Public Affairs Branch, U.S. Postal Service, 475 L'Enfant Plaza, SW, Washington, DC 20260-2175; or online at http://www.usps.gov/

Before your boss sends you on a foreign affair

The Overseas Security Advisory Council promotes security for businesses abroad. They have a data base and liaison staff which provides current unclassified threat information and directs you to local help in most areas of the world.

They have publications including *Security Guidelines for American Families Living Abroad* which outlines safety measures you can take and includes a videotape for kids.

Contact: Overseas Security Advisory Council, Bureau of Diplomatic Security, U.S. Department of State, Washington, DC 20522-1003; 202-663-0533; or online at http://ds.state.gov/publications.html

Security tips for the briefcase bunch

Personal Security Guidelines for the American Business Traveler Overseas recommends some precautionary measures for employees to take at the office and at home and suggests rules of behavior in a hostage situation.

Contact: Overseas Security Advisory Council, Bureau of Diplomatic Security, U.S. Department of State, Distribution Center, Washington, DC 20522-1003; 202-663-0533; or online at http://ds.state.gov/publications.html

Experts TRAC terrorists here

Think terrorist activities only happen in the Middle East? Think again. *Terrorism In The United States* is a free publication that lists the number of incidents that have occurred in the U.S. and analyzes current threats that exist.

Contact: TRAC Unit, Federal Bureau of Investigation, J. Edgar Hoover Bldg., Ninth St. and Pennsylvania Ave., NW, Room 5431, Washington, DC 20535; 202-324-2064; or online at http://www.fbi.gov/

Bombs and guns

Feel like you are living in the middle of a war zone? Find out what you are up against by requesting the following free publications:

Explosives Incidents Report (P3320.4) is an annual report, highlighting statistics of explosive incidents and stolen explosives and recoveries.

Identification of Firearms (5300.1) helps you in the identification of weapons, such as machine guns, rifles, and silencers. Just what you wanted to know!

Contact: Distribution Center, Bureau of Alcohol, Tobacco, and Firearms, U.S. Department of the Treasury, 7943 Angus Ct., Springfield, VA 22153; 703-455-7801; or online at http://www.atf.treas.gov/

Global terrorism tallied—get the free report

Every day we hear about a bombing or suspicious fire overseas. *Patterns of Global Terrorism*, published by the Office of Counter Terrorism, is a free annual report which provides statistical information, as well as analyses and chronology of significant terrorist events.

Contact: Office of Public Information, 2201 C St., NW, Room 6808, U.S. Department of State, Washington, DC 20520; 202-647-6575; or online at http://www.state.gov

Water questions

Is your cup half empty or half full? How much water is in that flood? How little water is there in the drought?

The Hydrologic Information Unit answers questions like these and more. They have a free monthly publication, *National Water Conditions*, which is a summary of water-resource conditions across the U.S.

Contact: Hydrologic Information Unit, U.S. Geological Survey, 419 National Center, Reston, VA 22092; 800-426-9000; or online at http://www.usgs.gov

It's your fault

If you really want to scare yourself silly, talk to the people at the Earthquake Information Center. They can answer all of your epicenter or seismic activity questions on earthquakes around the world.

To get free publications and answers to your earthquake questions contact: National Earthquake Information Center, U.S. Geological Survey, Mail Stop 967, Box 25046, Federal Center, Denver, CO 80225; 303-273-8500.

The worst winter in a hundred years

The weather has gotten very strange lately, and people are always predicting the worst. But it is better to be safe than sorry. The Federal Emergency Management Agency has produced several free publications on winter safety.

Child Disaster Preparedness Coloring Book (FEMA) includes safety precautions to be taken around the home before winter storms strike, and includes heating systems, room heaters and fireplaces, kitchen pipes, and emergency supplies.

Contact: Federal Emergency Management Agency, P.O. Box 70274, Washington, DC 20024; 800-480-2520; or online at http://www.fema.gov

The check's in the mail...or is it?

Worried about sending a birthday check to Junior?

A free booklet, *A Consumer's Guide to Postal Crime Prevention,* is full of helpful hints to discourage mail thieves. There is also information on how to deal with the problem of mail fraud.

Contact: Public Affairs Branch, The Postal Inspection Service, U.S. Postal Service, 475 L'Enfant Plaza, SW, Washington, DC 20260; 202-268-4293; or online at http://www.usps.gov/

When a disaster strikes

We all think we'd know what to do in an emergency, but in reality, planning is the key.

- *Family Earthquake Safety Home Hazard Hunt and Drill* (FEMA-113) discusses how to identify and correct hazards in the home and practice what to do if an earthquake occurs.

- *Hurricane Safety: Tips for Hurricanes* (L-105) provides helpful suggestions on what should be done in the event of a hurricane.

- *Tornado Safety Tips* (L-148) outlines safe behavior when a tornado strikes.

Contact: Federal Emergency Management Agency, P.O. Box 70274, Washington, DC 20024; 800-480-2520; or online at http://www.fema.gov

Insured, I'm sure

Some victims of the recent flood were covered under the government's National Flood Insurance Program (NFIP), but many were not. To find out if you qualify, get the free brochure, *Answers to Questions About The National Flood Insurance Program* which explains NFIP, and the type of assistance it provides.

For information on rules, regulations, claims, and publications, contact: National Flood Insurance Program, P.O. Box 6464, Rockville, MD 20849-6464; 800-638-6620; 800-480-2520 (publications); or online at http://www.fema.gov

First aid

Uncle Sam has a *First Aid Book* ($8) which recommends procedures for dealing with emergencies which require first aid. It includes sections on CPR, shock, wounds, burns, and more.

It also contains numerous illustrations, a bibliography, and an index, so be prepared!

For your copy contact: Superintendent of Documents, U.S. Government Printing Office, Washington, DC 20402: 202-512-1800; or online at http://www.gpo.gov/

You've survived the flood, now what?

Your home and its contents may look beyond hope, but many of your belongings can probably be restored.

Repairing Your Flooded Home is a free book published by the Federal Emergency Management Agency to help people who have been flooded and gives step-by-step advice you can use to clean up, rebuild, and get help after a flood.

For your copy contact: FEMA Publications, P.O. Box 70274, Washington, DC 20472; 202-646-3484; 800-480-2520; or online at http://www.fema.gov

Safe at any speed

Experiencing some car safety problems you feel are the manufacturer's fault?

The toll-free Auto Safety Hotline is your chance to help identify safety problems in motor vehicles, tires, and automotive equipment and also get safety information. Your complaint is logged and the manufacturer is notified.

If you are car or tire shopping, this hotline has a wealth of free information to help you with your decisions. *The Vehicle Crash Test Information* shows the relative crash protection provided front seat occupants in accidents at 35 mph. It also lists types of protection available and if anti-lock brakes are standard, optional, or available.

Regarding tires, the *Tire Quality Grading Report* provides information on the quality, mileage, and durability of various tires.

Contact: National Highway Traffic Safety Administration, Auto Safety Hotline NEF-11.2 HL, 400 Seventh St., SW, Washington, DC 20590; 800-424-9393; or online at http://www.nhtsa.dot.gov/

Army downsizing

Find out if the Army is downsizing, what the Defense Department budget is for this year as compared to previous years, and more through a free publication. *The Army Posture Statement* contains information on the Army's restructuring.

For your copies contact: U.S. Army Public Affairs, U.S. Department of Defense, The Pentagon, Washington, DC 20310; 703-697-7550; or online at http://www.army.mil/

Good news: Aviation accidents are down! Bad news: Fatalities are up!

Last year the number of aviation accidents dropped; however more people were killed than in the previous year. The National Transportation Safety Board (NTSB) reports a total of 1,013 people died in 2,229 aviation accidents either in the U.S. or involving U.S. registered civil aircraft last year.

These are just a few of the facts available in a free annual *End Report to Congress* from NTSB. Statistical information for the past ten years is also available.

Contact: National Transportation Safety Board, 490 L'Enfant Plaza, SW, Washington, DC 20594; 202-382-0660; or online at http://www.ntsb.gov/

A boss with itchy fingers

Are you having some trouble at work with your boss sexually harassing you?

To learn more about sexual harassment, you can contact the U.S. Equal Employment Opportunity Commission which has a series of publications on this topic, including:

- *Facts About Sexual Harassment*

- *Laws Enforced by the U.S. Equal Employment Opportunity Commission*

- *Questions and Answers About Sexual Harassment*

- *Sexual Harassment Resources*

For this and other information contact: Equal Employment Opportunity Commission, 1801 L St., NW, Washington, DC 20507; 202-663-4900; 800-669-4000; or online at http://www.eeoc.gov/ . To reach the publications information center, call 800-669-3362.

This is not a drill

No one thinks that a fire can happen to them, but it can. You need to know how to protect yourself and your family.

The U.S. Fire Administration has produced an array of free materials on such subjects as smoke detectors, alternate heater safety, characteristics of fire, and more.

Sesame Street Fire Safety Station is a program curricula for ages 3-10 designed to raise awareness about the subject of fire safety. *Let's Retire Fire* is a multi-dimensional program targeting senior Americans with vital safety messages. *An Ounce of Prevention* is a booklet providing information on automatic sprinklers and early warning systems. *Smoke Detectors: What You Need to Know* contains information on the importance, installation, and maintenance of smoke detectors.

Contact: Office of Fire Prevention and Arson Control, U.S. Fire Administration, 16825 South Seton Ave., Emmitsburg, MD 21727; 301-447-1660; or online at http://www.usfa.fema.gov/

On the wrong track

Information about railroad safety is available in a report known as the *Accident/Incident Bulletin,* which comes out annually.

There are three categories of reportable events; highway-rail accidents, train accidents, and any other event that results in a casualty. The report contains graphs and statistics.

For your free copy contact: U.S. Department of Transportation, Federal Railroad Administration, Office of Safety, 400 Seventh St., SW, Washington, DC 20591; 202-632-3386; or online at http://www.fra.dot.gov/

Nuclear fallout shelter plans

Want to build a snack bar that also serves as a nuclear fallout shelter? Two for the price of one!

The Federal Emergency Management Agency has several publications available at no charge to help you get started. Contact: Publications, Federal Emergency Management Agency, P.O. Box 70274, Washington, DC 20472, 800-480-2520; or online at http://www.fema.gov

Pipeline safety

One of the U.S. Department of Transportation's missions is in the area of pipeline safety. To see if and how this is being accomplished, you can get a free copy of the *Annual Report on Pipeline Safety.*

Contact: U.S. Department of Transportation, Research and Special Programs Administration, Washington, DC 20590; 202-366-4595; or online at http://ops.dot.gov/

Who's got the energy?

The Energy Information Administration is responsible for the collection, processing, and publication of data in the areas of energy resource reserves, technology, and much more.

A free *Energy Information Directory* is available which lists the amount of energy used, trends for future, and the outlook in the energy field.

Contact: U.S. Department of Energy, Energy Information Administration, 1000 Independence Ave., SW, Washington, DC 20585; 202-586-8800; or online at http://www.eia.doe.gov

Did I remember to turn off the ...

Whenever you go on a trip you always wonder if you turned off the coffee pot, iron, or stove.

Electrical safety is not to be taken lightly. The U.S. Consumer Product Safety Commission (CPSC) has put together a series of free publications dealing with electrical safety.

Some of the titles include:

• *Home Wiring Hazards*

• *Extension Cords Fact Sheet*

• *Electrical Receptical Fact Sheet*

• *Electrical Safety Room by Room Audit Checklist*

• *CPSC Home Electrical Safety Kit*

For your free copies or a complete publications list write: Publication Request, Office of Information and Public Affairs, U.S. Consumer Product Safety Commission, Washington, DC 20207; 800-638-2772; or online at http://www.cpsc.gov/

Is it safe here?

Choosing Where You Live is a consumer self help guide prepared by the U.S. Environmental Protection Agency. This guide offers publicly available information sources and guidelines for consumers to use when evaluating different geographic areas.

You can use this information in choosing the most appropriate environments for you to work, live, and play safely.

For a copy, contact: U.S. Environmental Protection Agency, Office of Air Quality Planning and Standards, Mail Drop 10, Research Triangle Park, NC 27711; 800-490-9198; or online at http://www.epa.gov/ttn/uatw/tolive.html

Save On Legal Fees

Fast answers to 90% of your legal questions

Clear, reliable & up-to-date

Save costly legal fees & protect your rights

More than a reference... a complete do-it-yourself tool!

Stock No.: BK311
$29.95 8.5" x 11"
500 pages Soft cover
ISBN 1-56382-311-X

Everyday Law Made E-Z

The book that saves legal fees every time it's opened.

Here, in *Everyday Law Made E-Z*, are fast answers to 90% of the legal questions anyone is ever likely to ask, such as:

• How can I control my neighbor's pet?
• Can I change my name?
• What is a common law marriage?
• When should I incorporate my business?
• Is a child responsible for his bills?
• Who owns a husband's gifts to his wife?
• How do I become a naturalized citizen?
• Should I get my divorce in Nevada?
• Can I write my own will?
• Who is responsible when my son drives my car?
• How can my uncle get a Green Card?
• What are the rights of a non-smoker?
• Do I have to let the police search my car?
• What is sexual harassment?
• When is euthanasia legal?
• What repairs must my landlord make?
• What's the difference between fair criticism and slander?
• When can I get my deposit back?
• Can I sue the federal government?
• Am I responsible for a drunken guest's auto accident?
• Is a hotel liable if it does not honor a reservation?
• Does my car fit the lemon law?

Whether for personal or business use, this 500-page information-packed book helps the layman safeguard his property, avoid disputes, comply with legal obligations, and enforce his rights. Hundreds of cases illustrate thousands of points of law, each clearly and completely explained.

MADE E-Z
PRODUCTS

Whatever you need to know we've made it E-Z!

Informative text and forms you can fill o on-screen.* From personal to business, le to leisure—we've made it E-Z!

PERSONAL & FAMILY

For all your family's needs, we have titles that will help keep you organized and guide you through most every aspect of your personal life.

BUSINESS

Whether you're starting from scratch with a home business or you just want to keep your corporate records in shape, we've got the programs for you.

E-Z to load, E-Z to run, E-Z to use!

BUSINESS STARTUPS MADE E-Z
PAYROLL MADE E-Z
PAYROLL MADE E-Z

For our complete list of titles, call 1-800-822-4566
or visit our web site: www.MadeE-Z.com

EVERYDAY LEGAL FORMS & AGREEMENTS MADE E-Z
BANKRUPTCY MADE E-Z
EVERYDAY LAW MADE E-Z
LIVING TRUSTS MADE E-Z
DIVORCE LAW MADE E-Z
LAST WILLS MADE E-Z

LEGAL

Easy to understand text explains how to fill out and file forms to perform all the legal tasks you need to—without all those legal fees!

TOURING LONDON, ENGLAND MADE E-Z
BRAIN-BUSTER CROSSWORD PUZZLES
AWARDS & CERTIFICATES MADE E-Z
CAR BUYING MADE E-Z
TOURING FLORENCE, ITALY MADE E-Z
BRAIN-BUSTER JIGSAW PUZZLES

TRAVEL & LEISURE

Learn health tips or travel all around the world, and then relax with a good crossword puzzle. When your work is done, we've got what you need!

MADE E-Z™
PRODUCTS

Made E-Z Products, 384 S. Military Trail, Deerfield Beach, FL 33442
(800) 822-4566 • fax: (954) 480-8906
web site: http://www.MadeE-Z.com

ss 1999.r2

FEDERAL & STATE
Labor Law Posters

CHECK OUT THE
MADE E·Z® LIBRARY

MADE E-Z GUIDES

Each comprehensive guide contain
the information you need to learn abou
of dozens of topics, plus sample forn
applicable).

Most guides also include an app
of valuable resources, a handy glo
and the valuable 14-page supple
"How to Save on Attorney Fees."

TITLES

Asset Protection Made E-Z
Shelter your property from financial disaster.

Bankruptcy Made E-Z
Take the confusion out of filing bankruptcy.

Buying/Selling a Business Made E-Z
Position your business and structure the deal for quick results.

Buying/Selling Your Home Made E-Z
Buy or sell your home for the right price right now!

Collecting Child Support Made E-Z
Ensure your kids the support they deserve.

Collecting Unpaid Bills Made E-Z
Get paid–and faster–every time.

Corporate Record Keeping Made E-Z
Minutes, resolutions, notices, and waivers for any corporation.

Credit Repair Made E-Z
All the tools to put you back on track.

Divorce Law Made E-Z
Learn to proceed on your own, without a lawyer.

Employment Law Made E-Z
A handy reference for employers and employees.

Everyday Law Made E-Z
Fast answers to 90% of your legal questions.

Everyday Legal Forms & Agreements Made E-Z
Personal and business protection for virtually any situation.

Incorporation Made E-Z
Information you need to get your company INC'ed.

Last Wills Made E-Z
Write a will the right way, the E-Z way.

Limited Liability Companies Made E-Z
Learn all about the hottest new business entity.

Living Trusts Made E-Z
Trust us to help you provide for your loved ones.

Living Wills Made E-Z
Take steps now to ensure Death with Dignity.

Managing Employees Made E-Z
Your own personnel director in a book.

Partnerships Made E-Z
Get your company started the right way.

Small Claims Court Made E-Z
Prepare for court...or explore other avenues.

Traffic Court Made E-Z
Learn your rights on the road and in court.

Solving IRS Problems Made E-Z
Settle with the IRS for pennies on the dollar.

Trademarks & Copyrights Made E-Z
How to obtain your own copyright or trademark.

Vital Record Keeping Made E-Z
Preserve vital records and important information.

KITS

Each kit includes a clear, concise instruction manual to help you understand your rights and obligations, plus all the information and sample forms you need.

For the busy do-it-yourselfer, it's quick, affordable, and it's E-Z.

	Item#	Qty.	Price Ea.‡
E♦Z Legal Kits			
ankruptcy	K100		$23.95
corporation	K101		$23.95
vorce	K102		$29.95
edit Repair	K103		$21.95
ving Trust	K105		$21.95
ing Will	K106		$23.95
st Will & Testament	K107		$18.95
ying/Selling Your Home	K111		$21.95
nployment Law	K112		$21.95
llecting Child Support	K115		$21.95
nited Liability Company	K116		$21.95
Made E♦Z Software			
counting Made E-Z	SW1207		$29.95
set Protection Made E-Z	SW1157		$29.95
nkruptcy Made E-Z	SW1154		$29.95
st Career Oppportunities Made E-Z	SW1216		$29.95
in-Buster Crossword Puzzles	SW1223		$29.95
in-Buster Jigsaw Puzzles	SW1222		$29.95
siness Startups Made E-Z	SW1192		$29.95
ving/Selling Your Home Made E-Z	SW1213		$29.95
Buying Made E-Z	SW1146		$29.95
porate Record Keeping Made E-Z	SW1159		$29.95
dit Repair Made E-Z	SW1153		$29.95
orce Law Made E-Z	SW1182		$29.95
ryday Law Made E-Z	SW1185		$29.95
ryday Legal Forms & Agreements	SW1186		$29.95
rporation Made E-Z	SW1176		$29.95
Wills Made E-Z	SW1177		$29.95
g Trusts Made E-Z	SW1178		$29.95
hore Investing Made E-Z	SW1218		$29.95
ing a Franchise Made E-Z	SW1202		$29.95
ing Florence, Italy Made E-Z	SW1220		$29.95
ing London, England Made E-Z	SW1221		$29.95
Record Keeping Made E-Z	SW1160		$29.95
site Marketing Made E-Z	SW1203		$29.95
Profitable Home Business	SW1204		$29.95
Made E♦Z Guides			
kruptcy Made E-Z	G200		$17.95
poration Made E-Z	G201		$17.95
rce Law Made E-Z	G202		$17.95
it Repair Made E-Z	G203		$17.95
g Trusts Made E-Z	G205		$17.95
g Wills Made E-Z	G206		$17.95
Wills Made E-Z	G207		$17.95
l Claims Court Made E-Z	G209		$17.95
c Court Made E-Z	G210		$17.95
g/Selling Your Home Made E-Z	G211		$17.95
oyment Law Made E-Z	G212		$17.95
cting Child Support Made E-Z	G215		$17.95
ed Liability Companies Made E-Z	G216		$17.95
erships Made E-Z	G218		$17.95
g IRS Problems Made E-Z	G219		$17.95
Protection Secrets Made E-Z	G220		$17.95
ration Made E-Z	G223		$17.95
g/Selling a Business Made E-Z	G223		$17.95
ade E♦Z Books			
ging Employees Made E-Z	BK308		$29.95
rate Record Keeping Made E-Z	BK310		$29.95
Record Keeping Made E-Z	BK312		$29.95
ess Forms Made E-Z	BK313		$29.95
ting Unpaid Bills Made E-Z	BK309		$29.95
day Law Made E-Z	BK311		$29.95
day Legal Forms & Agreements	BK307		$29.95
bor Posters			
al Labor Law Poster	LP001		$11.99
Labor Law Poster (specify state)			$29.95
PPING & HANDLING*			$
TAL OF ORDER**:**			$

See an item in this book you would like to order?

To order :
1. Photocopy this order form.
2. Use the photocopy to complete your order and mail to:

MADE E-Z PRODUCTS

384 S Military Trail, Deerfield Beach, FL 33442
phone: (954) 480-8933 ♦ fax: (954) 480-8906
web site: http://www.e-zlegal.com/

‡*Prices current as of 10/99*

Shipping and Handling: Add $3.50 for the first item, $1.50 for each additional item.

**Florida residents add 6% sales tax.

Total payment must accompany all orders.
Make checks payable to: Made E-Z Products, Inc.

NAME

COMPANY

ORGANIZATION

ADDRESS

CITY   STATE   ZIP

PHONE (   )

PAYMENT:

❑ CHECK ENCLOSED, PAYABLE TO MADE E-Z PRODUCTS, INC.

❑ PLEASE CHARGE MY ACCOUNT: ❑ MasterCard ❑ VISA

EXP.DATE

ACCOUNT NO.

Signature: _____
(required for credit card purchases)

-OR-

For faster service, order by phone:	*Or you can fax your order to us:*
(954) 480-8933	**(954) 480-8906**

ss 1999.r2